Not As Good as You Think
Why Middle-Class Parents in Colorado Should be Concerned About Their Local Public Schools

By Lance Izumi, J.D. with Alicia Chang Ph.D.

NOT AS GOOD AS YOU THINK
Why Middle-Class Parents in Colorado Should Be
Concerned about Their Local Public Schools
by Lance Izumi, J.D. with Alicia Chang, Ph.D.

September 2015

Pacific Research Institute
101 Montgomery Street, Suite 1300
San Francisco, CA 94104
Tel: 415-989-0833
Fax: 415-989-2411
www.pacificresearch.org

ISBN: 978-1-934276-22-8

Download copies of this study at www.pacificresearch.org.

Nothing contained in this report is to be construed as necessarily reflecting the views of the Pacific Research Institute or as an attempt to thwart or aid the passage of any legislation.

©2015 Pacific Research Institute. All rights reserved. No part of this publication may be reproduced, stored in a retrieval system, or transmitted in any form or by any means, electronic, mechanical, photocopy, recording, or otherwise, without prior written consent of the publisher.

Contents

Acknowledgements 7

Executive Summary 9

Introduction and Background on
"Not as Good as You Think" Research 13

Performance of Colorado Students on the National
Assessment of Educational Progress 14

Colorado Standards and Tests 17

Analysis of Individual Colorado Public Schools 20

Conclusions and Recommendations 35

Endnotes 41

Appendix 51

School Performance 51

About the Authors 116

About PRI 118

Acknowledgements

The authors would like to thank the Walton Family Foundation for its support of this project. We would like to thank James Lanich, Dave Johnston and the Educational Results Partnership for providing the data for the schools analysis. Also, we would like to thank Benjamin DeGrow, senior policy analyst at the Independence Institute's Education Policy Center, for peer-reviewing the draft of this study. In addition, we would like to thank Pam Benigno, director of the Education Policy Center at the Independence Institute, for her cooperation and assistance in the peer-review process. Any errors or omissions are the sole responsibility of the authors. The authors would like to thank PRI senior vice president Rowena Itchon for overseeing the publishing and marketing of the study. In addition, the authors would like to thank graphic designer Dana Beigel for her excellent layout of this study. The authors would like to acknowledge the contributions of Sally Pipes, president and CEO of PRI, and the rest of the dedicated staff of PRI. Finally, the authors would like to acknowledge the efforts of Chrissie Dong, formerly a member of PRI's development department, Ben Smithwick, director of development, and Laura Dannerbeck, director of events and marketing for PRI. The authors of this study have worked independently and their views and conclusions do not necessarily represent those of the board, supporters, or staff of PRI.

Executive Summary

Are regular Colorado public schools with predominantly non-low-income student populations performing well? Lots of middle-class parents think so and believe that education problems are limited to places such as inner-city Denver. Yet, based on a variety of indicators, many of these schools may not be as good as parents think they are.

On the National Assessment for Educational Progress (NAEP), often referred to as the nation's report card, many non-low-income Colorado students fail to perform at the targeted proficient level:

- On the 2013 NAEP fourth-grade reading test, 45 percent of non-low-income Colorado test-takers failed to score at proficient level.
- On the NAEP fourth-grade math test, 35 percent of non-low-income Colorado students failed to score at the proficient level.
- On the 2013 NAEP eighth-grade reading exam, 48 percent of non-low-income Colorado test-takers failed to score at the proficient level.
- On the NAEP eighth-grade math exam, 45 percent of non-low-income Colorado test-takers failed to score at the proficient level.

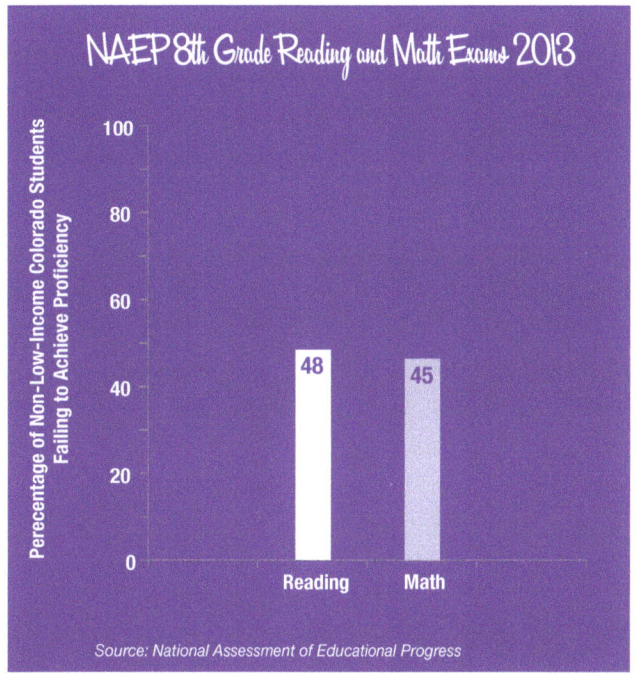

Non-low-income Colorado students also have lower proficiency rates on the NAEP compared to similar students in top-performing states such as Massachusetts, and have roughly similar proficiency rates to students in neighboring Kansas.

Prior to the new Common Core-aligned exam, the state-administered exam in Colorado was the Transitional Colorado Assessment Program (TCAP), which was used in grades 3-10. Research comparing TCAP scores and scores of Colorado students on the NAEP have found that it is much easier to achieve proficiency on TCAP than on NAEP. Thus, seemingly high proficiency rates on TCAP should be viewed with a grain of salt—those rates may not indicate the true knowledge and preparation level of Colorado students.

In Colorado, there are 479 regular public schools where 33 percent or fewer of their students are classified as low income, i.e. schools with predominantly non-low-income student populations. Among these schools, 103, or 22 percent, have 50 percent or more of their students in at least one grade level failing to meet or exceed proficiency on the 2014 TCAP. Much of the underperformance is concentrated at the high-school level.

Among the 103 predominantly non-low-income high schools in Colorado, 77, or 75 percent, had at least one grade-level math or reading exam where 50 percent or more of their students failed to reach proficiency. Virtually all of these grade-level failures were in mathematics, which indicates that many Colorado middle-class students may not be receiving adequate preparation for STEM learning in college and STEM-related jobs in the marketplace

Many schools with more than 50 percent of their students in at least one grade level failing to meet or exceed proficiency on a subject-matter exam (mostly on state math exams) are in middle-class neighborhoods.

At Fort Collins High School in Fort Collins, which was once named by a national magazine as the best place to live in America, 53 percent of ninth-graders failed to score at or above the proficient level on the 2014 ninth-grade Transitional Colorado Assessment Program (TCAP) math exam. On the tenth-grade TCAP math exam, 60 percent of Fort Collins High test-takers failed to hit the proficient mark.

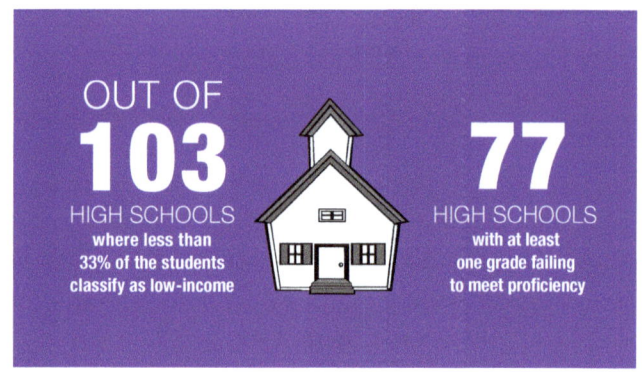

Other predominantly middle-class regular public schools with student proficiency problems include, but are not limited to:

- Hemphill Middle School in Adams County
- Broomfield High School in Broomfield County
- Monarch High School in Boulder County
- Castle View High School in Douglas County
- Pine Creek High School in El Paso County
- Green Mountain High School in Jefferson County
- Miller Middle School in La Plata County
- Rocky Mountain High School in Larimer County
- Parkview Elementary School in Rio Blanco County
- Windsor High School in Weld County

These results should cause non-low-income Colorado parents, many of whom are middle class, to rethink their views on the quality of their neighborhood public schools, and, consequently, to open their minds to other education options, choices and policy changes that would allow their children to escape underperforming schools and attend better-performing alternatives. Among these alternatives are a variety of school-choice programs:

- Colorado should consider a universal tax-credit program. Illinois has enacted a universal tax-credit program that allows individuals to claim tax credits for educational expenses, such as private-school tuition.
- The Denver-based Independence Institute has proposed a dollar-for-dollar tax credit to individuals or businesses that contribute to qualified nonprofit organizations that provide scholarships for K-12 non-public tuition.
- Nevada has enacted a groundbreaking first-in-the-nation law making education savings accounts (ESAs) available to all parents and their children. The state will deposit funding into ESAs that parents can use for private-school tuition, online education, tutoring or other education services.

Increased choice for parents of all income levels, therefore, should be the guiding principle for Colorado policymakers. Too many children in Colorado, including many from middle-class families, are underperforming in the core subjects. They have an inherent right to be able to attend a better school, whether public or private.

Introduction and Background on "Not as Good as You Think" Research

In 2007, the Pacific Research Institute (PRI) published a landmark book entitled *Not as Good as You Think: Why the Middle Class Needs School Choice*. The book examined student performance on California math and English exams in the state's public schools that had relatively few low-income students. The book found that hundreds of these public schools were underperforming based on the California Standards Test (CST). In 2009, PRI published a follow-up study entitled "Still Not as Good as You Think: Why the Middle Class Needs School Choice." This current study examines schools with similar student populations in Colorado to discover whether the same phenomenon is occurring.

In the 2007 PRI book, the authors examined the pool of schools in California where a third or fewer of the students at the school were eligible for the National School Lunch Program (NSLP), which is the federal program that provides free or reduced-priced lunches to students. Participation in the NSLP program is often used as a proxy for student socioeconomic status. Children from families with incomes at or below 130 percent of the poverty level are eligible for free meals, and those from families with incomes between 130 percent and 185 percent of the poverty level are eligible for reduced-price meals. If only a third or fewer of the students at a school were eligible for the NSLP program, one could reasonably conclude that predominantly non-low-income or non-economically-disadvantaged students attended the school.

Using the benchmark of one-third or fewer students eligible for the NSLP is a very conservative categorization. For example, a study by the Third Way think tank attempted to examine student achievement at middle-class public schools around the country. The study used a broad definition of "middle class" —"Those with between 26 percent and 75 percent eligibility [for the NSLP] represent our target middle-class schools."[1] The study's authors, however, acknowledged some problems with the wide net that they cast: "There are some characteristics in which the schools with 51-75 percent of their student population eligible for the NSLP look more like lower-income schools than middle-class schools."[2] Given such an admission, our more conservative approach seems prudent.

Within the pool of public schools with one-third or fewer students eligible for the NSLP program, PRI's 2007 book then examined the performance on the state-standards-aligned California Standards Test (CST) in mathematics and English. California had set grading benchmarks of advanced, proficient, basic, below basic, and far below basic. It was the state's goal that all students score at least at the proficient level on the CST. The authors then reviewed the test results from the pool of predominantly non-low-income schools and determined how many schools had more than 50 percent of students performing below proficiency in at least one grade level on either the CST math or English exam. For this result to occur, even if every low-income student in a grade level at a school performed below the proficient mark on a grade-level test, a significant percentage of non-low-income students also had to perform below proficiency.

Based on these criteria, the 2007 book found almost 300 public schools in California with predominantly non-low-income student populations where more than half of the students in at least one grade level failed to reach proficiency in either math or English on the state exam.[3]

This current study uses the 33/50 criteria and applies it to regular public schools in Colorado.[4] The Colorado Department of Education equates "economic disadvantaged" status with eligibility for the National School Lunch Program.[5]

Performance of Colorado Students on the National Assessment of Educational Progress

There are several ways to address the question of how well non-low-income students in Colorado are performing. To get a big picture of the achievement of Colorado's non-low-income students, one of the first places to which researchers turn is to the state's results on the National Assessment of Educational Progress (NAEP).

Often referred to as the nation's report card, the NAEP exams are used in virtually all states and test students periodically in several subjects:

> Students are tested in a variety of different subject areas and grade levels, and they are scored as either achieving advanced, proficiency, basic or below basic in a specific subject. The Commissioner of Education Statistics, under the U.S. Department of Education, is responsible for overseeing the NAEP. The National Assessment Governing Board, an independent, bipartisan board appointed by the Secretary of Education, is responsible for determining the framework and assessments given. The Board also defines basic, proficient, and advanced levels for each grade.
>
> Achieving 100 percent proficiency on NAEP exams is a goal that all schools should be striving for.[6]

In defining "proficiency," the U.S. Department of Education states: "This level represents solid performance for each grade assessed," and that students reaching the proficient level "have demonstrated competency over challenging subject matter, including subject matter knowledge, application of such knowledge to real world situations, and analytical skills appropriate to the subject matter."[7] In contrast, to achieve a "basic" level, a student need display only partial mastery of perquisite knowledge and skills that are fundamental for proficient work at that grade level. Colorado, like most other states, participates in NAEP testing.

Paul Peterson of Harvard University and Fredrick Hess of the American Enterprise Institute (AEI) have written that the difficulty level of NAEP's test items and its definition of "proficiency" have been judged to be on par with the standards used by designers of international tests of student achievement. "Proficiency," they conclude, "has acquired roughly the same meaning in Europe and Asia, and in the United States—as long as the NAEP standard is employed."[8]

NAEP uses matrix sampling, a testing technique that assembles different assessment documents covering different aspects of a subject. These different assessments are administered to different sample sets of students. In other words, on the NAEP reading exam not every student answers the same questions. Aggregate scores for all students are then calculated.[9]

Since NAEP uses matrix sampling, it is impossible to compare scores between students or between schools. This situation is unlike state tests, such as the Transitional Colorado Assessment Program (TCAP), which allows for such comparisons, since all students in a given grade level take the same test and answer the same questions. NAEP produces statewide data and allows for comparisons of performance between states and gives a picture of statewide student performance.

The most recent NAEP results show that Colorado has not only failed to come close to the 100-percent proficiency goal for all students, the state has also failed to come close to this proficiency goal for non-low-income students, who are often assumed to be higher achieving.

NAEP scores can be broken down into various group categories, including by participation and non-participation in the NSLP. On the 2013 NAEP fourth-grade reading exam, 45 percent of Colorado students not eligible for the NSLP failed to score at the proficient level.[10] Non-low-income Colorado fourth graders did better in math, with 35 percent failing to score at or above the proficient level on the NAEP fourth-grade math exam.[11] The results, however, were worse for non-low-income Colorado eighth graders.

On the 2013 NAEP eighth-grade reading exam, 48 percent of non-low-income Colorado students, nearly half, failed to score at or above the proficient level.[12] Forty-five percent of non-low-income Colorado eighth graders failed to score at or above proficiency on the NAEP math exam.[13]

NAEP identifies "advanced" as signifying "superior performance."[14] On the 2013 fourth-grade NAEP reading and math exams, 84 percent of Colorado non-NSLP-eligible test takers failed to reach the advanced level.[15] On the eighth-grade NAEP reading exam, 93 percent of non-low-income Colorado test-takers failed to achieve the advanced level.[16] On the eighth-grade math exam, 82 percent of non-low-income test-takers failed to make the advanced level.[17]

Not only has the achievement level of non-low-income students in Colorado failed to approach the 100-percent proficiency goal, it also compares unfavorably with the performance of similar students in other states. For example, Massachusetts is ranked among the leaders in NAEP performance, and its non-low-income students significantly outperform their peers in Colorado.

On the 2013 NAEP fourth-grade math exam, 26 percent of non-low-income students in Massachusetts failed to reach proficiency versus 35 percent in Colorado.[18] On the fourth-grade reading exam, 38 percent of non-low-income test-takers in Massachusetts failed to hit proficiency, while 45 percent of non-low-income Colorado test-takers failed to do so.[19] There were similar disparities on the eighth-grade NAEP exams.

On the eighth-grade NAEP math exam, 31 percent of non-low-income students in Massachusetts failed to hit the proficiency mark, while 45 percent of non-low-income Colorado eighth-graders failed to achieve proficiency.[20] On the eighth-grade reading exam, 39 percent of non-low-income students in Massachusetts failed to score at the proficient level, while 48 percent of non-low-income Colorado students failed to achieve proficiency.[21]

Colorado's non-low-income students performed at roughly the same level as non-low-income students in neighboring Kansas. On the 2013 fourth-grade NAEP math exam, 37 percent of Kansas non-low-income students failed to score at or above the proficient level, while 35 percent of Colorado non-low-income test-takers failed to do so.[22] On the fourth-grade reading exam, 46 percent of non-low-income Kansas test-takers failed to hit proficiency, while 45 percent of non-low-income Colorado test-takers failed to hit that mark.[23]

On the 2013 eighth-grade math exam 46 percent of non-low-income students in Kansas failed to score at or above proficiency, while 45 percent of non-low-income Colorado eighth graders failed to achieve proficiency.[24] On the eighth-grade reading exam, 52 percent of non-low-income students in Kansas failed to score at the proficient level, while 48 percent of non-low-income Colorado students failed to achieve proficiency.[25]

To be fair, it should be pointed out that higher percentages of non-low-income students in Colorado perform at the proficient level on the 2013 NAEP exams than other states examined in PRI's "Not as Good as You Think" series of studies. For example, on the fourth-grade NAEP math exam, 43 percent of Michigan non-low-income test-takers failed to reach the proficiency level, while 35 percent of Colorado non-low-income students failed to hit the proficiency mark. On the fourth-grade NAEP reading exam, 56 percent of Michigan non-low-income students failed to reach proficiency versus 45 percent in Colorado.

On the eighth-grade NAEP math exam, 58 percent of non-low-income students in Michigan failed to hit the proficiency mark, while 45 percent of non-low-income Colorado eighth-graders failed to achieve proficiency. On the eighth-grade reading exam, 55 percent of non-low-income students in Michigan failed to score at the proficient level, while 48 percent of non-low-income Colorado students failed to achieve proficiency.[26]

Nevertheless, not only are large proportions of non-NSLP-eligible Colorado students failing to achieve proficiency on NAEP exams, they are failing to match the proficiency rates of their peers in leading states like Massachusetts or significantly exceed the rates in neighboring states such as Kansas. However, to understand the full extent of the underperformance of non-NSLP-eligible Colorado students, one must analyze their performance on Colorado's state exams.

Colorado Standards and Tests

Any discussion of state testing must first start with an examination of the rigor of a state's subject-matter standards. States with challenging and rigorous subject-matter standards will usually have rigorous tests since state tests are aligned with state standards. Thus, prior to the advent of the national Common Core education standards, states such as California and Massachusetts had their own rigorous individual state standards, plus standards-aligned tests that also were considered rigorous. In Colorado, the state's pre-Common Core state standards, the Colorado Academic Standards (CAS), which were adopted by the Colorado State Board of Education in December 2009, received mixed reviews.

The Thomas B. Fordham Institute has been grading state subject-matter standards for years. In its 2010 report on state standards, Fordham gave California an "A" and Massachusetts an "A-" for their English-language-arts (ELA) standards. Colorado's ELA standards received a respectable "B+" grade. According to the Fordham Institute report, Colorado's ELA standards are "thoughtful" and cover content in "useful ways."[27]

The group's report judged the Colorado's ELA standards to be better than the Common Core national standards in literary and non-literary text analysis, logic, and oral presentation[28] In contrast, Colorado's math standards did not rate well.

The Fordham report gave Colorado's math standards a mediocre "C" grade. In comparison, California's state math standards received an "A+," while Massachusetts received a "B+" for its math standards. In its evaluation, the Fordham reviewers also said that arithmetic is "not adequately developed" in Colorado's math standards and that high school material "misses a good deal of essential content."[29]

Colorado's high school math standards were especially lacking. According to the Fordham report:

> High school content is often weak. The coverage of linear equations is missing some essential details, including equations for parallel and perpendicular lines. The coverage of quadratics is also incomplete. Quadratics is not developed coherently, and specific mention of it is infrequent. . . .
>
> Missing content includes complex roots, vertex form, and max/min problems.
>
> While factoring is mentioned, polynomials are not, and the arithmetic of polynomials and rational functions is not covered.
>
> Much of the STEM-ready content is also missing, including inverse trigonometric functions and polar coordinates.[30]

Fordham concluded that the Common Core math standards were superior to Colorado's pre-Common Core state math standards.[31]

The Colorado State Board of Education adopted the Common Core national education standards in ELA and mathematics in August 2010. In December 2010, the Colorado Department of Education released a new version of the CAS for mathematics, reading, writing and communication, which incorporated the entire Common Core national education standards into the CAS.[32]

In 2013 and 2014, Colorado's state exam in reading and mathematics was the Transitional Colorado Assessment Program (TCAP). According to the Colorado Department of Education, "Where possible, TCAP has been designed to measure standards that are common between the old standards and the new standards." TCAP was designed to be used for two years, after which Colorado started to use the national Common Core test designed by the Partnership for Assessment for College and Careers (PARCC). TCAP assessed students in math and reading in grades three through 10.[33] This study uses TCAP data from 2014.

The TCAP has four different performance levels. According to the Colorado Department of Education, these include:

> Advanced (Level 4). A student scoring at the Advanced Level has success with the most challenging content of the [standards]. These students answer most of the test questions correctly, including the most challenging questions.
>
> Proficient (Level 3). A student scoring at the Proficient Level has success with the challenging content of the [standards]. These students answer most of the test questions correctly, but may have only some success with questions that reflect the most challenging content.
>
> Partially Proficient (Level 2). A student scoring at the Partially Proficient Level has limited success with the challenging content of the [standards]. These students may demonstrate inconsistent performance, answer many of the test questions correctly but are generally less successful with questions that are most challenging.
>
> Unsatisfactory (Level 1). A student scoring at the Unsatisfactory Level has little success with the challenging content of the [standards].[34]

Ideally, all students should score at or above the proficient mark. These definitions, however, do not tell students, parents and the public about the level of difficulty of TCAP.

How rigorous is the TCAP? Other states studied by the authors, such as Illinois and Michigan, have state reading and math exams that are far from rigorous, which allows many students to achieve a proficient score when their real level of knowledge is much less developed. One way to see how Colorado's test stacks up is to compare scores on the state tests with scores on NAEP.

A May 2015 report by the Washington, DC-based education organization Achieve analyzed the disparity between scores on state tests and the 2013 NAEP. According to the report:

> Frequently, states' testing and reporting processes yield significantly different results than the data collected and reported by the National Assessment of Educational Progress (NAEP). While NAEP, the Nation's Report Card, scores are the gold standard for measuring student achievement and serve as a yardstick for state comparisons, NAEP

results are generally not known by students and their families who rely on their state test results to know how they are performing. While no single test can show everything we need to know about how a student is performing in school, test scores along with information about a student's work in the classroom give families the information they need to know about a student's progress.[35]

When comparing test scores and student proficiency rates on state tests with scores and rates by students in each state on NAEP, the report found: "Too many states are saying students are 'proficient' when they are not actually well prepared." Colorado, for the most part, falls into this conclusion.

In fourth-grade reading, 26 percent more Colorado students scored "proficient" on the TCAP than on the 2013 NAEP. In fourth-grade math, 22 percent more Colorado students scored "proficient" on the TCAP than on the NAEP.[36]

In eighth-grade reading, 27 percent more Colorado students scored "proficient" on the TCAP than on the NAEP. In eighth-grade math, 9 percent more Colorado students scored "proficient" on the TCAP than on NAEP.[37]

The Achieve report's findings indicate that there was a large gap between the performance of Colorado students on the TCAP versus their performance on the NAEP. This gap shows that gaining proficiency on TCAP was significantly easier than achieving proficiency on NAEP. Thus, seemingly high proficiency rates on TCAP should be viewed with a grain of salt – those rates may not indicate the true knowledge and preparation level of Colorado students.

Finally, it should be pointed out that Colorado also has an analytical mechanism called the Colorado Growth Model (CGM). The CGM is a statistical model to calculate each student's progress on assessments and is a tool for displaying student, school and district results to educators and the public. Specifically, the CGM shows:

- how individual students (and groups of students) progress from year to year toward state standards. Each student's progress is compared to the progress of other students in the state with a similar score history on CSAP in that subject area.
- the observed growth among different groups of students at the state, district, and school level.
- the level of growth that we needed to observe in order to say that students were, on average, on track to catch up or keep up (Adequate Growth).
- schools and districts that produce the highest rates of growth in academic achievement. These schools or districts may not be ones with the highest test scores every year - growth level is completely independent of achievement level for individual students.[38]

The CGM is a very important and useful tool for analyzing student and school performance. However, for the purposes of this study, results on the 2014 TCAP will be used.

Analysis of Individual Colorado Public Schools

The 33/50 Schools

As was mentioned previously, NAEP scores are useful in giving a big-picture statewide check on student achievement, but they cannot be used to evaluate individual school performance. Given that limitation, there are other ways to analyze the performance of individual Colorado public schools.

This study employs the methodology used in the 2007 PRI *Not as Good as You Think* book, which focused on public schools with 33 percent or fewer of students on the National School Lunch Program (NSLP) and 50 percent or more of students in at least one grade level that failed to achieve proficiency on the state tests. Since California's standards were very rigorous, the state tests were also challenging and resulted in many schools with predominantly non-low-income students failing to meet that threshold. In view of the inflated proficiency rates on the TCAP vis-à-vis the NAEP, fewer predominantly middle-class Colorado schools have 50 percent or more of their students failing to reach proficiency in at least one grade level in reading or math than would be the case if the TCAP were a more rigorous exam. However, despite TCAP's comparative lack of rigor, a significant number of predominantly non-low-income Colorado schools still meet the *Not as Good as You Think* benchmark.

Based on the 2014 TCAP results, out of 479 regular Colorado public schools with predominantly non-low-income student populations, 103, or 22 percent, had at least one grade-level state math or reading exam where 50 percent or more of their students failed to reach proficiency. Much of the underperformance is concentrated at the high-school level and in mathematics.

Among the 103 predominantly non-low-income high schools in Colorado, 77, or 75 percent, had at least one grade-level math or reading exam where 50 percent or more of their students failed to reach proficiency. Virtually all of these grade-level failures were in mathematics, which indicates that many Colorado middle-class students may not be receiving adequate preparation for STEM learning in college and STEM-related jobs in the marketplace.

The poor math performance of non-low-income students can be seen in schools across Colorado. The following are some examples of the Colorado schools that are not as good as you would think.

Adams County

Horizon High School is located in Thornton, which is 10 miles from downtown Denver. In 2013, Thornton had a population of 127,356, a 54 percent increase over the population in 2000, which made the city the sixth most populous in Colorado. Named after former Colorado governor Dan Thornton, the city was the first fully planned community in Adams County.

The median household income in Thornton in 2012 was $60,972, which was 7 percent higher than the statewide median of $56,765. The median home value in the city was $194,800, which was 17 percent lower than the statewide median of $234,900.[39]

In 2013, Horizon High School had 1,900 students, with whites constituting 67 percent and Hispanics constituting 24 percent. Eighteen percent of Horizon High students, less than two in 10, were categorized as economically disadvantaged.[40]

On the ninth-grade 2014 TCAP math exam, 53 percent of Horizon students failed to achieve proficiency. On the tenth-grade TCAP math exam, 60 percent of Horizon students failed to score at or above the proficient level.

Hemphill Middle School is located in Strasburg, which is about 25 miles outside Aurora. Strasburg,

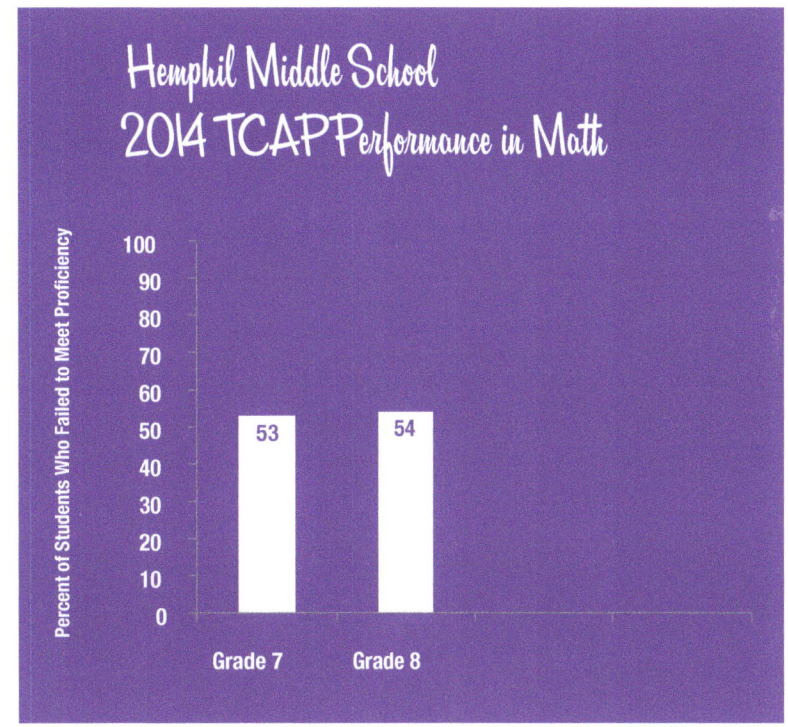

with a population of 2,447 in 2010, is best known as the place where the last link in the coast-to-coast rail network in the United States was completed in 1870.

The median household income in Strasburg in 2012 was $73,591, which was 30 percent higher than the statewide median of $56,765. The median home value in the town was $193,388, which was 18 percent lower than the statewide median of $234,900.[41]

In 2013, Hemphill Middle School had 214 students, with whites constituting 91 percent of the student population and Hispanics constituting 7 percent. Less than one in four students, 23 percent, were classified as economically disadvantaged.[42]

On the seventh-grade 2014 TCAP math exam, 53 percent of Hemphill students failed to score at or above the proficient level. On the eighth-grade TCAP math exam, 54 percent of Hemphill students failed to hit the proficient mark.

If Hemphill Middle School in Strasburg is having problems in math, it is no surprise that students at Strasburg High School are also having similar problems.

In 2012-13, Strasburg High had an enrollment of about 320 students, with whites constituting 83 percent of the student population and Hispanics constituting 13 percent. Thirteen percent of students are classified as economically disadvantaged.[43]

On the ninth-grade 2014 TCAP math exam, 77 percent of Strasburg High students failed to score at or above the proficient level. On the tenth-grade TCAP math exam, 83 percent of Strasburg students failed to hit the proficient mark.

Arapahoe County

Cherokee Trail High School is in Aurora, which had a 2013 population of 345,803, which made the city the third most populous in Colorado. Aurora is a suburb of Denver and makes up part of the Denver-Aurora-Lakewood metropolitan statistical area. Aurora is home to Buckley Air Force Base, which is the largest employer in the city. U.S. Secretary of State John Kerry was born in an Army hospital in Aurora in 1943. In 2004, *Sports Illustrated* magazine named Aurora as "Sportstown" for Colorado.

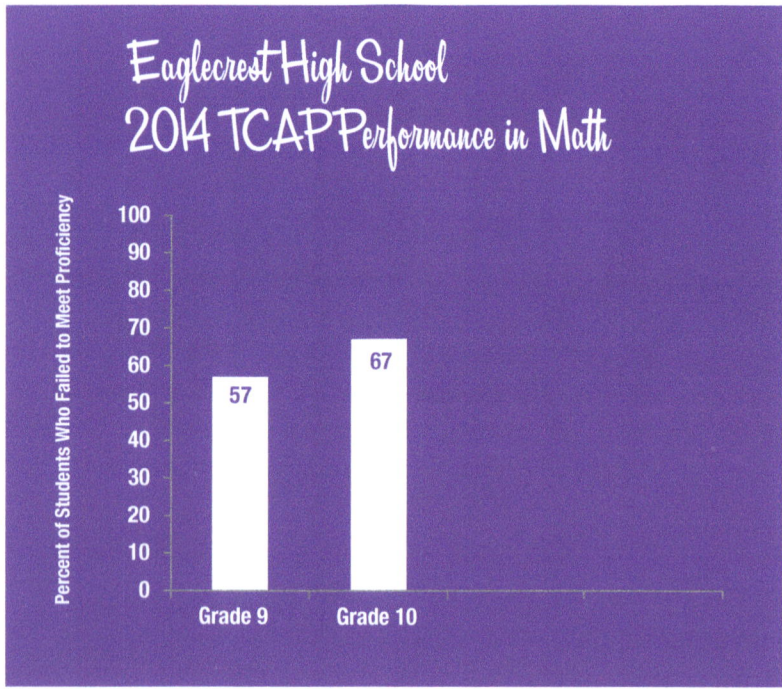

The median household income in Aurora in 2012 was $50,512, which was 11 percent lower than the statewide median of $56,765. The median home value in the city was $177,000, which was 25 percent lower than the statewide median.

In 2013, Cherokee Trail High School had 2,550 students, with whites constituting 59 percent of the student population, Hispanics constituting 14 percent, African Americans constituting 12 percent, and Asian Americans constituting 9 percent. Thirteen percent of the school's students were categorized as economically disadvantaged.[44]

On the tenth-grade 2014 TCAP math exam, 59 percent of Cherokee Trail tenth-graders, six out of 10, failed to score at or above the proficient level.

Eaglecrest High School is located just outside Centennial, which had a 2013 population of 106,114, which made it the tenth most populous city in Colorado. Centennial is less than 10 miles outside of Aurora.

The median household income in Centennial in 2012 was $59,524, which was 5 percent higher than the statewide median of $56,765. The median home value in the city was $244,412, which was 4 percent higher than the statewide median of $234,900.[45] The city website says that Centennial has been ranked as one of the best places to live by *USA Today* and *Money* magazine.[46]

In 2013, Eaglecrest High School had a student population of roughly 2,400, with whites constituting 55 percent, Hispanics constituting 19 percent, African Americans constituting 15 percent, and Asian Americans constituting 7 percent. About one in four students, 26 percent, were classified as economically disadvantaged.[47]

Parent reviews of Eaglecrest High are mostly positive. One parent says, "My son graduated from here – AMAZING teachers and administration." Talking about the age of the school's facilities, the same parent urges, "Don't judge a book by its cover."[48] Parents at Eaglecrest should take this admonishment to heart and look at how students are faring academically at the school.

On the ninth-grade 2014 TCAP math exam, 57 percent of Eaglecrest High students failed to score at or above the proficient level. On the tenth-grade TCAP math exam, two-thirds of Eaglecrest test-takers, 67 percent, failed to hit the proficient mark.

Boulder County

Monarch High School is located in Louisville, which had a 2013 population of 19,588. Originally a mining town, Louisville has been named multiple times as one of the best places to live in the nation by *Money* magazine. Louisville lies a few miles outside of Boulder and West Adams.

The median household income in Louisville in 2012 was $84,466, which was 49 percent higher than the statewide median of $56,765. The median home value in the city was $383,214, which was 63 percent higher than the statewide median of $234,900.[49]

In 2013, Monarch High School had a student population of roughly 1,600, with whites constituting 80 percent and Hispanics constituting 9 percent. Less than 8 percent were classified as economically disadvantaged.[50]

Monarch High had been awarded with excellence awards in years past, including being named by *Newsweek* magazine as one of the country's best high schools. However, on the 2014 tenth-grade TCAP math exam, 51 percent of Monarch High test-takers failed to score at or above the proficient level.

Silver Creek High School is located in Longmont, which had a 2013 population of 89,919. Longmont is northeast of Boulder and 33 miles from Denver. Astronaut Vance Brand, who was the command module pilot for the first U.S.-Soviet joint spaceflight in 1975 and the commander of three Space Shuttle missions, lived in Longmont. The local airport is named in his honor.

The median household income in Longmont in 2012 was $58,789, which was 4 percent higher than the statewide median of $56,765. The median home value in the city was $249,600, which was 6 percent higher than the statewide median of $234,900.[51]

In 2013, Silver Creek High School had a student population of roughly 1,000, with whites constituting 80 percent and Hispanics constituting 15 percent. Just 15 percent were classified as economically disadvantaged.[52]

On the tenth-grade 2014 TCAP math exam, 52 percent of Silver Creek High students failed to score at or above the proficient level.

Broomfield County

Broomfield High School is located in the city of Broomfield, which had a population in 2013 of 59,471, which was a 55 percent increase over the population in 2000. Named for broomcorn that was grown in the region, the city of Broomfield is in Broomfield County, Colorado's newest county, which was established in 2001.

The median household income in Broomfield in 2012 was $79,036, which was 40 percent higher than the statewide median of $56,765. The median home value in the city was $276,587, which was 18 percent higher than the statewide median of $234,900.[53]

In 2013, Broomfield High School had a student population of roughly 1,400, with whites constituting 78 percent and Hispanics constituting 13 percent. Thirteen percent were classified as economically disadvantaged.[54]

On the ninth-grade 2014 TCAP math exam, 54 percent of Broomfield High students failed to score at or above the proficient level. On the tenth-grade TCAP math exam, 56 percent of Broomfield test-takers failed to hit the proficient mark.

Douglas County

Castle View High School is located in the city of Castle Rock, which had a population in 2013 of 53,063, which was an amazing 162 percent increase over the population in 2000. Named for a prominent castle-shaped butte near the center of town, Castle Rock is the most populous municipality in Douglas County and is located midway between Denver and Colorado Springs. *Money* magazine, *Family Circle* magazine and *Forbes* have all named Castle Rock as one of the best places to live in America.

The median household income in Castle Rock in 2012 was $79,931, which was 41 percent higher than the statewide median of $56,765. The median home value in the city was $270,881, which was 15 percent higher than the statewide median of $234,900.[55]

In 2013, Castle View High School had a student population of roughly 1,700, with whites constituting 79 percent and Hispanics constituting 15 percent. Just 12 percent were classified as economically disadvantaged.[56] Parent reviews of Castle View High are mixed.

While some parent say that their children have had positive experiences at the school, others complain about the lack of help for struggling students. One parent commented:

> This is probably one of the worst schools my daughter has ever attended. The teachers are not helpful and neither is administration. If your child is not gifted or just needs some extra help, forget about it. It's either keep up or get left behind and forgotten. I will be taking her out before the end of the year.[57]

Another parent concluded: "Bottom line, either plan to go to a private or charter school if you want quality or send your kids out of district."[58] Based on the school's math scores, parents worried about educational quality seem to have a valid concern.

On the ninth-grade 2014 TCAP math exam, 51 percent of Castle View High students failed to score at or above the proficient level. On the tenth-grade TCAP math exam, 58 percent of Castle View test-takers failed to hit the proficient mark.

Douglas County High School is also located in Castle Rock. Famed Academy Award-nominated actress Amy Adams graduated from Douglas County High.

In 2013, Douglas County High had a student population of roughly 1,900, with whites constituting 76 percent and Hispanics constituting 15 percent. Thirteen percent were classified as economically disadvantaged.[59]

Posted reviews of the school are mixed. One student voicing a very negative opinion wrote:

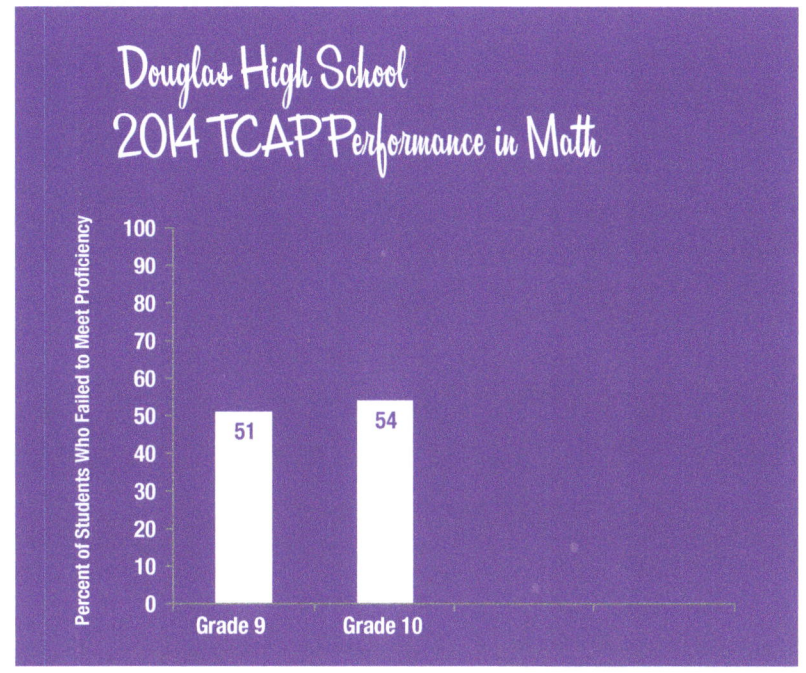

> After one year at this high school, I believe there is an extreme amount of room for improvement. The staff and administration are very unhelpful most of the time, and the classes are exceptionally easy. This school's main focus is on its athletics, not its academics.[60]

On the ninth-grade 2014 TCAP math exam, 51 percent of Douglas County High students failed to score at or above the proficient level. On the tenth-grade TCAP math exam, 54 percent of Douglas County High test-takers failed to hit the proficient mark.

Chaparral High School is located in Parker, which had a 2013 population of 48,608, which was an eye-opening 106 percent increase over 2000. Parker is a commuter suburb in the Denver area. Dana Perino, who served as President George W. Bush's press secretary at the end of his second term, grew up in Parker.

The median household income in Parker in 2012 was $90,148, which was 59 percent higher than the statewide median of $56,765. The median home value in the city was $281,091, which was 20 percent higher than the statewide median of $234,900.[61]

In 2013, Chaparral High School had a student population of more than 2,000, with whites constituting 78 percent and Hispanics constituting 12 percent. Just 11 percent were classified as economically disadvantaged.[62]

On the tenth-grade 2014 TCAP math exam, 54 percent of Chaparral High students failed to score at or above the proficient level.

Mountain Vista High School is located in Highlands Ranch, which had a 2010 population of 96,713, which was a 36 percent increase over the population in 2000. A suburb of Denver, Highlands Ranch is one of the most populous unincorporated communities in the United States. Golden Globe Award-winning actress Keri Russell lived for a period in Highlands Ranch.

The median household income in Highlands Ranch in 2012 was $98,580, which was 74 percent higher than the statewide median of $56,765. The median home value in the city was $327,700, which was 40 percent higher than the statewide median of $234,900.[63]

In 2013, Mountain Vista High School had a student population of roughly 2,100, with whites constituting 80 percent and Hispanics constituting 10 percent. A miniscule 6 percent were classified as economically disadvantaged.[64]

On the tenth-grade 2014 TCAP math exam, 52 percent of Mountain Vista High students failed to score at or above the proficient level.

El Paso County

Liberty High School is located in Colorado Springs, which had a 2013 population of 439,886, which made the city the second most populous in the state behind Denver. Colorado Springs is situated at the base of Pikes Peak and is home to the U.S. Olympic Training Center, the Pro Rodeo Hall of Fame, the United States Air Force Academy, plus a number of other prominent military installations, including the North American Aerospace Defense Command (NORAD).

The median household income in Colorado Springs in 2012 was $52,622, which was 7 percent lower than the statewide median of $56,765. The median home value in the city was $210,400, which was 10 percent below than the statewide median of $234,900.[65]

In 2013, Liberty High School had a student population of roughly 1,500, with whites constituting 75 percent and Hispanics constituting 13 percent. Just 11 percent were classified as economically disadvantaged.[66]

On the tenth-grade 2014 TCAP math exam, 53 percent of Liberty High students failed to score at or above the proficient level.

Pine Creek High School is also located in Colorado Springs. In 2013, Pine Creek High School had a student population of roughly 1,400, with whites constituting 79 percent and Hispanics constituting 10 percent. A tiny 5 percent were classified as economically disadvantaged.[67]

One parent posts that Pine Creek High is the "Best school in the state."[68] Pine Creek is not the best school in math, however.

On the tenth-grade 2014 TCAP math exam, 52 percent of Pine Creek High students failed to score at or above the proficient level.

Another underperforming Colorado Springs high school is Rampart High. In 2013, Rampart High had a student population of roughly 1,600, with whites constituting 68 percent, Hispanics constituting 15 percent, and Asian Americans constituting 7 percent. Only 12 percent were classified as economically disadvantaged.[69]

On the ninth-grade 2014 TCAP math exam, 50 percent of Rampart High students failed to score at or above the proficient level. On the tenth-grade TCAP math exam, 53 percent of Rampart High test-takers failed to hit the proficient mark.

Vista Ridge High School is also in Colorado Springs. In 2013, Vista Ridge High had a student population of roughly 1,200, with whites constituting 60 percent, Hispanics constituting 20 percent, and African Americans constituting 11 percent. Eighteen percent, fewer than two in 10 students, were classified as economically disadvantaged.[70]

Posted comments by parents are largely negative. One parent writes, "My child has joined the ranks of the functionally illiterate." Another parent says: "This district & school pass kids onto the next grade regardless of if they pass their core courses. My son has graduated by the skin of his teeth yet he doesn't deserve to."[71]

On the ninth-grade 2014 TCAP math exam, 57 percent of Vista Ridge High students failed to score at or above the proficient level. On the tenth-grade TCAP math exam, an eyebrow-raising 70 percent of Vista Ridge High test-takers failed to hit the proficient mark.

Manitou Springs High School is located in the city of Manitou Springs, which had a population in 2013 of 5,245. Founded as a scenic health resort, with a still functioning mineral springs, Manitou Springs continues to be a tourist destination for hikers and day-tripping families. Ultra-marathoner Matt Carpenter has won the Pikes Peak Marathon, which begins in Manitou Springs and climbs to the top of the peak, an amazing 12 times.

The median household income in Manitou Springs in 2012 was $47,444, which was 16 percent lower than the statewide median of $56,765. Paradoxically, the median home value in the city was $328,461, which was 40 percent higher than the statewide median of $234,900.[72]

In 2013, Manitou Springs High School had a student population of roughly 500, with whites constituting 84 percent and Hispanics constituting 10 percent. Nineteen percent, fewer than two in 10 students, were classified as economically disadvantaged.[73]

On the ninth-grade 2014 TCAP math exam, 59 percent of Manitou Springs High students failed to score at or above the proficient level. On the tenth-grade TCAP math exam, a too-high 71 percent of

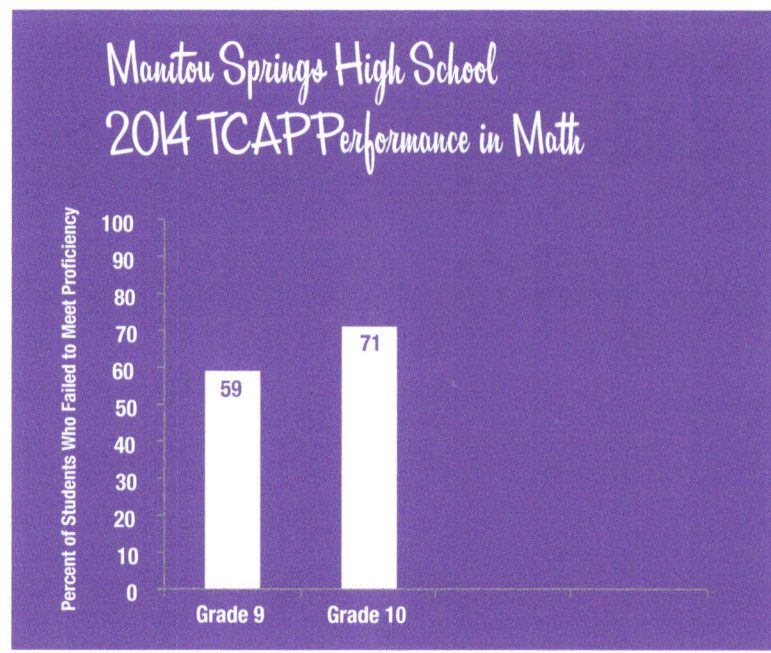

Manitou Springs High test-takers failed to hit the proficient mark.

Elbert County

Elizabeth High School is located in the town of Elizabeth, which had a population in 2013 of 1,373. The most populous municipality in Elbert County, the town is a bedroom community for the Denver metro area.

The median household income in Elizabeth in 2012 was $55,096, which was roughly equivalent to the statewide median of $56,765. The median home value in the city was $185,202, which was 21 percent lower than the statewide median of $234,900.[74]

In 2013, Elizabeth High School had a student population of roughly 800, with whites constituting 86 percent and Hispanics constituting 10 percent. Less than 15 percent, fewer than two in 10 students, were classified as economically disadvantaged.[75]

Parent reviews of the school are generally positive. In one recent post, a parent wrote:

> I am a parent of two. One freshman and one Junior. I have been very happy with EHS. My kids are challenged and for such a small community, there are lots of course offerings. The teachers, though relatively low paid, care immensely about the kids. Learning takes place here. Much better than the schools in bigger cities. So glad we moved here.[76]

Yet, despite such praise, the school's test scores indicate areas of deficiency.

On the ninth-grade 2014 TCAP math exam, 57 percent of Elizabeth High students failed to score at or above the proficient level. On the tenth-grade TCAP math exam, 64 percent of Elizabeth High test-takers failed to hit the proficient mark.

Jefferson County

Green Mountain High School is located in the city of Lakewood, which had a population in 2013 of 147,214. Lakewood is west of Denver and is the most populous city in Jefferson County and the fifth most populous city in Colorado. In 2011, the National Civic League named Lakewood as an "All-American City."

The median household income in Lakewood in 2012 was $53,967, which was just under the statewide median of $56,765. The median home value in the city was $244,300, which was 4 percent higher than the statewide median of $234,900.[77]

In 2013, Green Mountain High School had a student population of roughly 1,100, with whites constituting 75 percent and Hispanics constituting 18 percent. Less than one in four students, 24 percent, were classified as economically disadvantaged.[78]

On the ninth-grade 2014 TCAP math exam, 50 percent of Green Mountain High students failed to score at or above the proficient level. On the tenth-grade TCAP math exam, 58 percent of Green Mountain High test-takers failed to hit the proficient mark.

Golden High School is located in Golden, the county seat of Jefferson County. Golden is in the foothills of the Rockies and had a 2013 population of 19,393, which was a 13 percent increase over the city's population in 2000. The popular Jolly Rancher candy was born in Golden, Coors beer has the largest single-site brewery in the world located in the town, and famed western showman "Buffalo Bill" Cody is buried near Golden.

The median household income in Golden was nearly the same as the statewide median. The median home value in the city in 2013 was $368,019, which was 57 percent above the statewide median.

In 2013, Golden High School had a student population of roughly 1,200, with whites constituting 79 percent and Hispanics constituting 13 percent. A little more than one in four students, 27 percent, were classified as economically disadvantaged.[79]

On the ninth-grade 2014 TCAP math exam, 53 percent of Golden High students failed to score at or above the proficient level. On the tenth-grade TCAP math exam, 58 percent of Golden High test-takers failed to hit the proficient mark.

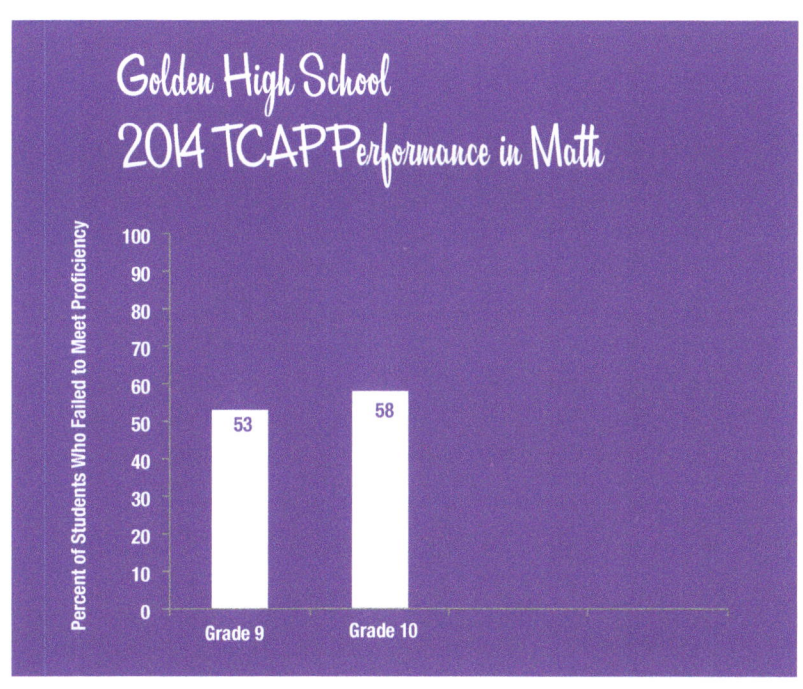

Standley Lake High School is located in Westminster, which had a 2013 population of 110,945, which was a 10 percent increase over the city's population in 2000. Westminster is a northwest suburb of Denver and is the seventh most populous city in Colorado. In the mid-2000s, *Money* magazine ranked Westminster as the 24th best place to live in the United States.

In 2013, Standley Lake High School had a student population of roughly 1,400, with whites constituting 69 percent, Hispanics constituting 17 percent and Asians constituting 8 percent. Thirty percent, three out of 10 students, were classified as economically disadvantaged.[80]

On the ninth-grade 2014 TCAP math exam, 55 percent of Standley Lake High students failed to score at or above the proficient level. On the tenth-grade TCAP math exam, 59 percent of Standley Lake High test-takers failed to hit the proficient mark.

La Plata County

Durango High School is located in the city of Durango, which had a population in 2013 of 17,557, which was a 26 percent increase over the population in 2000. Founded by the Denver and Rio Grande Railroad, Durango is the county seat and most populous municipality in La Plata County. The city is a popular destination spot for those seeking outdoor activities such as hiking, mountain biking, rafting, kayaking, fishing and golfing. A haven for foodies, Durango has more restaurants per capita than Denver. Steve Carlton, one of the greatest pitchers in Major League Baseball history, lives in Durango.

The median household income in Durango in 2012 was $51,823, which was 9 percent lower than the statewide median of $56,765. The median home value in the city was $354,830, which was 51 percent higher than the statewide median of $234,900.[81]

In 2013, Durango High School had a student population of roughly 1,200, with whites constituting 75 percent and Hispanics constituting 17 percent. Less than one in four students, 23 percent, were classified as economically disadvantaged.[82]

Posted comments by Durango High students indicate a variety of problems at the school. Typical is this post by a student in 2015:

> Absolutely the worst school I have been to. It is full of drugs and I was not challenged academically whatsoever. The foreign language program was very poor. The teachers do not make an effort to properly teach. Their attendance policy is horrid, they let kids skip whenever they want. I went there for a year and I was not challenged and didn't learn anything. Do not send your kids here if you want them to excel.[83]

While a harsh judgment, the school's poor math scores bolster this student's criticisms.

On the ninth-grade 2014 TCAP math exam, 53 percent of Durango High students failed to score at or above the proficient level. On the tenth-grade TCAP math exam, 60 percent of Durango High test-takers failed to hit the proficient mark.

Also in Durango is Miller Middle School. In 2013, Miller Middle School had a student population of roughly 1,200, with whites constituting 76 percent and Hispanics constituting 16 percent. Less than three in 10 students, 29 percent, were classified as economically disadvantaged.[84]

Student performance at Miller seems to decrease as the grades go onward. On the 2014 sixth-grade

TCAP math exam, 37 percent of Miller students failed to score at or above the proficient level. On the seventh-grade TCAP math exam, the percentage of students failing to hit the proficiency benchmark rises to 46 percent. And on the eighth-grade 2014 TCAP math exam, 51 percent of Miller Middle School students failed to score at or above the proficient level.

Larimer County

Berthoud High School is located in the town of Berthoud, which had a 2013 population of 5,394, which was a 12 percent increase over the population in 2000. Berthoud sits about halfway between Fort Collins and Denver. The farmland around Berthoud is nicknamed the "Garden Spot of Colorado."

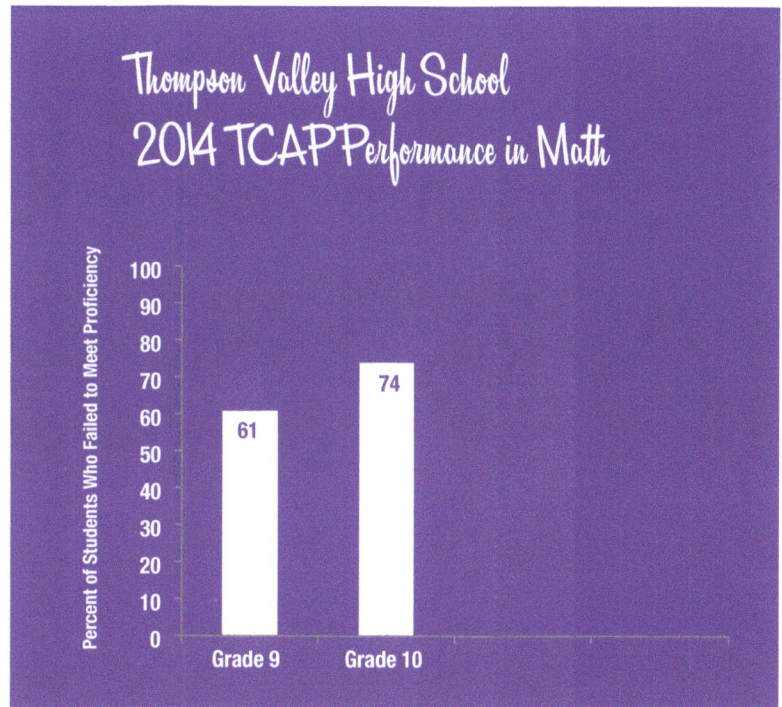

The median household income in Berthoud in 2012 was $67,829, which was 19 percent higher than the statewide median of $56,765. The median home value in the city was $227,206, which was 3 percent lower than the statewide median of $234,900.[85]

In 2013, Berthoud High School had a student population of roughly 650, with whites constituting 86 percent and Hispanics constituting 10 percent. Less than two out of 10 students, 19 percent, were classified as economically disadvantaged.[86]

Parent reviews of Berthoud High are mixed. One parent complimented Berthoud as a "very math and science oriented school."[87] Perhaps so, but math test scores indicate problems.

On the ninth-grade 2014 TCAP math exam, 51 percent of Berthoud High students failed to score at or above the proficient level.

Thompson Valley High School is located in the city of Loveland, which had a population in 2013 of 71,334, which was a 26 percent increase over the population in 2000. Loveland is just south of Fort Collins and 46 miles north of Denver. Publications such as *USA Today* and *Money* magazine have named the Fort-Collins-Loveland metropolitan area as great places to live. Olympic gold medal-winning cyclist Alexi Grewal has lived in the Loveland area.

The median household income in Loveland in 2012 was $56,798, which was virtually the same as the statewide median of $56,765. The median home value in the city was $209,600, which was 11 percent lower than the statewide median of $234,900.[88]

In 2013, Thompson Valley High School had a student population of roughly 1,300, with whites constituting 83 percent and Hispanics constituting 13 percent. Less than three out of 10 students, 28 percent, were classified as economically disadvantaged.[89]

Posted comments by parents are generally positive. One parent wrote that Thompson Valley High was a "fantastic school to prepare students for college."[90] Yet, the school's most recent math scores seem to contradict such praise.

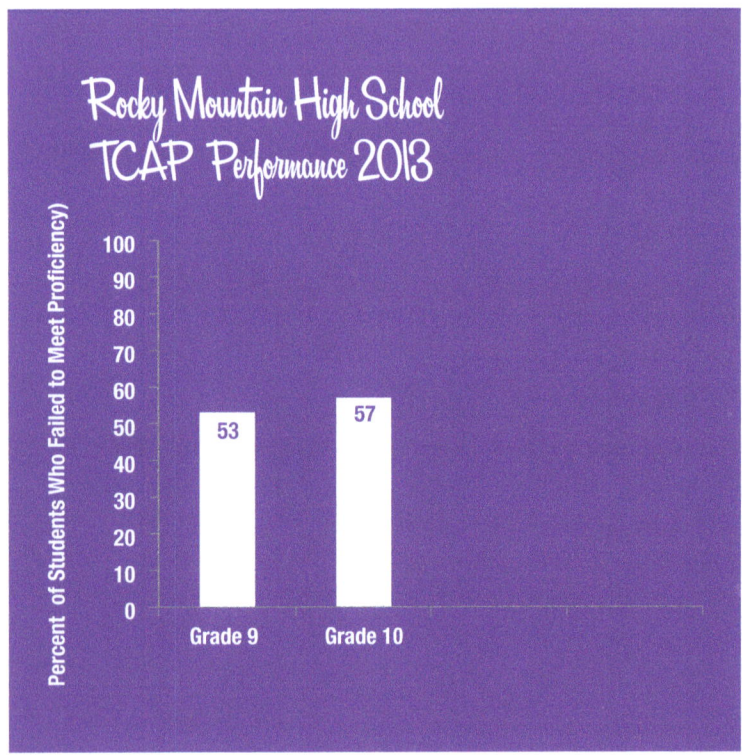

On the ninth-grade 2014 TCAP math exam, 61 percent of Thompson Valley High students failed to score at or above the proficient level. On the tenth-grade TCAP math exam, three-quarters of Thompson Valley High test-takers, 74 percent, failed to hit the proficient mark.

Rocky Mountain High School is in Fort Collins, which had a 2013 population of 152,061, which was a 28 percent increase over the city's population in 2000. In the mid-2000s, *Money* magazine ranked Fort Collins as the best place to live in America. The magazine said, "great schools, low crime, good jobs in a high-tech economy and a fantastic outdoor life make Fort Collins No. 1."[91]

In 2013, Rocky Mountain High School had a student population of roughly 2,000, with whites constituting 78 percent and Hispanics constituting 14 percent. Just more than one out of four students, 27 percent, were classified as economically disadvantaged.[92]

On the ninth-grade 2014 TCAP math exam, 53 percent of Rocky Mountain High students failed to score at or above the proficient level. On the tenth-grade TCAP math exam, 57 percent of Rocky Mountain High test-takers failed to hit the proficient mark.

Also in Fort Collins is Fort Collins High School. In 2013, Fort Collins High had a student population of roughly 1,600, with whites constituting 69 percent and Hispanics constituting 23 percent. Twenty-nine percent of students were classified as economically disadvantaged.[93]

On the ninth-grade 2014 TCAP math exam, 53 percent of Fort Collins High students failed to score at or above the proficient level. On the tenth-grade TCAP math exam, 60 percent of Fort Collins High test-takers failed to hit the proficient mark.

Rio Blanco County

Parkview Elementary School is located in the town of Rangely, which had a 2013 population of 2,433, which was a 16 percent increase over the population in 2000. On the far western side of the state, the town is home to Colorado Northwestern Community College and is near several important sites of the ancient Fremont Native American people. Oil, coal and natural gas production are the main drivers of economic activity in the area.

The median household income in Rangely in 2012 was $68,930, which was 21 percent higher than the statewide median of $56,765. The median home value in the city was $169,826, which was 28 percent lower than the statewide median of $234,900.[94]

In 2013, Parkview Elementary had a student population of roughly 330, with whites constituting 86 percent and Hispanics constituting 12 percent. About two out of 10 students, 21 percent, were classified as economically disadvantaged.[95]

On the fifth-grade 2014 TCAP math exam, 58 percent of Parkview Elementary students failed to score at or above the proficient level.

San Miguel County

Telluride High School is located in the famed ski town of Telluride, which had a 2013 population of 2,319. Home to the Telluride Ski Resort, the town is also popular with mountain bikers, hikers and river rafters. Major Hollywood stars show up for the Telluride Film Festival.

The median household income in Telluride in 2012 was $62,559, which was 10 percent higher than the statewide median of $56,765. The median home value in the city was $906,369, which was 286 percent higher than the statewide median of $234,900.[96]

In 2013, Telluride High had a student population of roughly 210, with whites constituting 75 percent and Hispanics constituting 21 percent. Fewer than one in four students, 24 percent, were classified as economically disadvantaged.[97]

On the tenth-grade 2014 TCAP math exam, 54 percent of Telluride High students failed to score at or above the proficient level.

Summit County

Summit High School is located in the town of Frisco, which had a 2013 population of 2,319. The town is located near four major ski resorts: Copper Mountain, Breckenridge, Keystone, and Arapahoe Basin. Like other ski towns in Colorado, Frisco is popular in non-winter months for its outdoor activities such as hiking, fishing, kayaking, rafting, camping and golfing.

The median household income in Frisco in 2012 was $72,102, which was 27 percent higher than the statewide median of $56,765. The median home value in the city was $482,299, which was 105 percent higher than the statewide median of $234,900.[98]

In 2013, Summit High had a student population of roughly 740, with whites constituting 72 percent and Hispanics constituting 23 percent. About two out of 10 students, 22 percent, were classified as economically disadvantaged.[99]

On the tenth-grade 2014 TCAP math exam, 56 percent of Summit High students failed to score at or above the proficient level.

Weld County

Windsor High School is located in the city of Windsor, which had a population in 2013 of 20,422, which was a 106 percent increase over the population in 2000. Windsor is located 60 miles north of Denver in the Northern Colorado region, and is halfway between Fort Collins and Greeley. Originally known for its sugar beets, Windsor has been successful in attracting green industries, including wind blade production, ethanol production and recycling facilities.

The median household income in Windsor in 2012 was $78,207, which was 38 percent higher than the statewide median of $56,765. The median home value in the city was $261,089, which was 11 percent higher than the statewide median of $234,900.[100]

In 2013, Windsor High School had a student population of roughly 1,200, with whites constituting 80 percent and Hispanics constituting 14 percent. Sixteen percent were classified as economically disadvantaged.[101]

On the ninth-grade 2014 TCAP math exam, 51 percent of Windsor High students failed to score at or above the proficient level. On the tenth-grade TCAP math exam, more than two-thirds of Windsor High test-takers, 68 percent, failed to hit the proficient mark.

Conclusions and Recommendations

What this paper has shown is that many non-low-income students in Colorado are underperforming. These performance issues can be seen using a variety of measurements.

On the NAEP exams, large proportions of non-low-income Colorado students fail to perform at the proficient level. Also, Colorado trails high-performing states like Massachusetts and does little better than neighboring states like Kansas in the proportion of non-low-income students performing at proficiency on the NAEP.

Of the 479 regular public schools in Colorado that have 33 percent or fewer of their students designated as low income, 103, or 22 percent, have at least one grade where 50 percent or more of students in that grade level failed to meet or exceed the proficient level on either the state's TCAP reading or math test.

Among the 103 predominantly non-low-income high schools in Colorado, 77, or 75 percent, had at least one grade-level math or reading exam where 50 percent or more of their students failed to reach proficiency. Virtually all of these grade-level failures were in mathematics

These results should cause middle-class Colorado parents to re-think their views on the quality of their neighborhood public schools, and, consequently, to open their minds to other education options, choices, and policy changes that would allow their children to escape underperforming schools and attend better-performing alternatives.

It is no secret that many middle-class parents decide to locate to certain neighborhoods because they think that the local public schools are high performing and will benefit their children. Former Harvard Law professor and current U.S. Senator Elizabeth Warren and her daughter Amelia Warren Tyagi have written that the major reason middle-class families are willing to shell out so much of their incomes on housing is that "when a family buys a house, it buys much more than shelter from rain"; rather, it "buys a public-school system." They note, "For most middle-class parents, ensuring that their children get a decent education means buying a home in a small subset of well-reputed school districts."

Warren and Tyagi advise: "Any policy that loosens the ironclad relationship between location-location-location and school-school-school would eliminate the need for parents to pay an inflated price for a home just because it happens to lie with the boundaries of a desirable school district."[102] Such a policy would "relieve parents from the terrible choice of leaving their kids in lousy schools or bankrupting themselves to escape those schools."[103]

Toby Young, who has written a book on free schools, which are the British version of U.S. charter schools, has pointed out that many middle-class schools in Britain are underperforming. Yet, in many areas in Britain, like in Colorado, there is only one government-run public school for miles around "so the only choice is to plump for the local school or go private."[104] Given the cost of private education, Young says:

> For middle-income or low-income families, that isn't any choice at all. It's the lack of any competition that enables these "sink" middle-class schools to "muddle through." After all, the vast majority of parents in the surrounding areas will have no choice but to send their children to these schools, regardless of how poorly they perform.[105]

For middle-class parents, who have gone into debt to buy into "good" neighborhoods with "good" public schools, what are they to do when they find out that the schools are not as good as they thought they were? The answer is to consider and support school-choice programs that are not just targeted at small groups of low-income families, but that give parents of all or most income levels the ability to choose the public or private school that best meets the needs of their children.

For besieged middle-class parents, Warren and Tyagi recommended, "A well-designed voucher program would fit the bill neatly."[106] As *The New Yorker* has pointed out, Warren supports public-school vouchers, where parents could send their children to any public school.[107] Colorado has a long-running open enrollment program known as the Public Schools of Choice law.

Under the open enrollment program, students may enroll at schools in districts for which they are not zoned. In other words, students may attend public schools other than their neighborhood public schools. There are restrictions, however:

> Students may open enroll into any public school as long as certain criteria are met. Most schools that do not have room for more students will have a waiting list. When there is room for more students, schools will either accept students on a first-come-first-served basis or hold a lottery to determine which students may enroll in the school.[108]

Thus, while the open enrollment program does give parents and their children some measure of choice, that choice is still limited by space availability. The limitations of the open enrollment program argue for the creation and implementation of other choice options.

For the time being, one such option, vouchers to pay for private religious schools, is off the table for Colorado parents. In June 2015, the Colorado Supreme Court ruled against the school-choice voucher program enacted by Douglas County in 2011. In a 4-3 decision, the court said that the Douglas County program, which created a limited number of vouchers available for parents of all income levels that could be used to pay for tuition at private independent and parochial schools, violated the state constitution's Blaine Amendment. That provision prevents government aid to religious institutions.

The state high court's decision is especially unfortunate given the performance problems of a number of Douglas County schools, as noted earlier in this study. County parents hoping to use the vouchers to find better quality education for their children are sadly out of luck.

While vouchers for most current private schools are off the policy table for now, there are other tools that can potentially increase the ability of Colorado parents to choose the best schooling for their children.

Tax Credits

Tax credit programs that allow individuals to claim tax credits for educational expenses, such as private-school tuition, can offer middle-class parents an immediate way to escape underperforming public schools and send their children to more suitable private schools. Such tax credits can also help parents afford tutoring and other assistance if switching to another school is not possible.

According to Jason Bedrick of the Cato Institute and Lindsey Burke of the Heritage Foundation, tax-credit laws have a "perfect record of constitutionality thus far." In 2011, the U.S. Supreme Court rejected a challenge to Arizona's tax-credit law because the funds did not become public money since they had "not come into the tax collector's hands."[109]

A previous study in this "Not as Good as You Think" series, which focused on Illinois, highlighted that state's tax credit program. According to The Friedman Foundation's description of the Illinois program:

> Parents receive a tax credit worth 25 percent of their expenditures after the first $250, up to a maximum credit of $500 per family. To get the maximum $500 credit, parents must spend $2,250 on educational expenses; they must also have a state tax liability of at least $500 because the credit is nonrefundable and thus cannot reduce an individual's tax burden to less than zero.
>
> Educational expenses must be for students who are residents of Illinois, who are younger than 21, and have attended kindergarten through 12th grade in a public or private school in Illinois or were homeschooled.[110]

The great aspect of the Illinois educational tax-credit program is that it is available to all Illinois taxpayers regardless of income level. Yet, as The Friedman Foundation points out, the program is hampered by some key shortcomings:

> Illinois' individual tax credit could be one of the country's most effective choice programs if it made some updates. On student eligibility, the program is accessible to all students statewide. Moreover, there are no unreasonable regulations placed on private schools. Those strong features are hurt, however, by the fact that participants have very little funding power with a maximum available credit of just $500. Illinois could improve this program dramatically by raising the tax credit allowance to at least the state's average per-pupil expenditure in public schools and providing a refundable credit (similar to Alabama) so that low-income families can participate.[111]

If the value of the Illinois tax credit was raised, many more parents, including middle-class parents, could take advantage of the program and send their children to private schools that better meet their needs. An Illinois-style tax-credit program, with a higher credit level, is something that Colorado policymakers should consider.

Another type of tax-credit program would give taxpayers a dollar-for-dollar tax credit for money they donate to a nonprofit organization that then offered scholarships to students to attend private schools.

Thus, a person with a $1,000 state tax bill, who makes a $400 donation to a scholarship organization, would see his or her tax bill reduced to $600. Seven of the 17 tax-credit scholarship programs in the country provide a dollar-for-dollar 100 percent credit for all donations.

A 2014 report by the Denver-based Independence Institute advocates just such a tax-credit program: "A model program would provide dollar-for-dollar tax credits to persons or businesses that contribute to qualified nonprofit organizations that provided scholarships for K-12 non-public tuition." Specifically, the report, authored by Benjamin DeGrow, senior education policy analyst at the Independence Institute, recommends:

- All children from families with incomes at or below 300 percent of federal poverty level should be eligible for a scholarship.

- To promote cost savings, scholarship eligibility during the program's first three years further should be limited to students previously enrolled in public school, incoming kindergarteners or 1st graders, new state residents, and students already receiving a tuition scholarship.

- The average scholarship amount issued by a participating nonprofit organization should be set at 50 percent of state average Per Pupil Revenue ($7,023 in fiscal year 2014-15).

- The program ideally should operate without a total annual program cap. If a reasonably sized cap is implemented, it should include a mechanism for automatic annual cap increases.

- The program should limit credits for individual contributions to a taxpayer's total liability.

- Participating nonprofit organizations must abide by basic financial account-ability standards and must disburse at least 90 percent of their funds as scholarships, though the General Assembly also could consider a relaxed standard for startup organizations.

- Using one of a selection of nationally norm-referenced tests, participating private schools would report scholarship students' academic progress to an independent research organization for a publicly reported annual evaluation.[112]

While the plan proposed by the Independence Institute would not benefit all middle-class families, its eligibility provision would allow some non-low-income families to have access to the scholarships:

> Tax credit scholarships primarily should be available to families with the least financial means, but not made so restrictive as to exclude others who cannot reasonably afford private school tuition. Ideally, students from low- or middle-income households that are already eligible for enrollment in Colorado public K-12 schools should be likewise able to receive a scholarship for non-public school tuition. Scholarships should be extended to families earning as much as 300 percent of the federal poverty rate, currently $59,370 a year for a family of three.[113]

The report estimates that "roughly half of families – the least affluent – would be eligible to receive the benefit."[114]

Education Savings Accounts

Education savings accounts are another school-choice alternative that may or may not survive a Blaine Amendment challenge in Colorado.

An ESA program, according to the Friedman Foundation, "allows parents to withdraw their children from public, district, or charter schools and receive a portion of their public funding deposited into an account with defined, but multiple, uses, including private school tuition, online education, private tutoring, or future educational expenses."[115]

Bedrick and Burke have written that ESAs have two important advantages over school-choice vouchers:

> In addition to being able to direct ESA funds to multiple providers and products, parents can save unused funds from year to year and roll the funds into a college savings account. These two features of ESAs — the ability of parents to completely customize their child's education and save for future educational expenses — make them distinct from and improvements upon traditional school vouchers. Parents have the ability to maximize the value their children get from their education services, and, because they control how and when the money is spent, they have a greater incentive to control costs, too.[116]

In June 2015, Nevada Governor Brian Sandoval signed groundbreaking first-in-the-nation legislation that will make education savings accounts (ESAs) available to all parents and their children. These advantages are clearly seen in Nevada's new ESAs.

Under Nevada's new program, for parents earning above the low-income level, the state will deposit funds, totaling 90 percent of the average statewide support per pupil, or roughly $5,100, into ESAs starting next year. For parents earning below the low-income level or who have children with special needs, the state will deposit 100 percent of the average statewide support per pupil, around $5,700, into parents' ESAs. Parents can then withdraw funds from their ESAs to pay for a variety of educational services such as private-school tuition, distance-learning online programs, and tutoring. Any funds that are not spent in a school year will be allowed to roll over year to year until the student is no longer eligible to be enrolled in a public school.[117]

The universality of Nevada's ESA program sets it apart from all other ESA efforts. Glenn Cook, a senior editorial writer at the *Las Vegas Review-Journal*, has written:

> ESAs exist in Arizona, Florida, Tennessee and Mississippi, but they place restrictions on eligibility. Across the country, parents only gain the power of choice based on their income or whether their child's school performs poorly. Nevada's ESA law only requires that students first be enrolled in public school to take advantage.[118]

Bedrick and Burke are cautious in judging whether ESAs can survive legal challenges based on state Blaine Amendments. However, they point out that Arizona has made the distinction between vouchers and ESAs:

> Where ESAs entail the allocation of public funds, they may not withstand scrutiny in states where courts have adopted very restrictive interpretations of the Blaine amendment. Nevertheless, the example of Arizona is encouraging on this point for advocates of ESAs. Despite having previously struck down vouchers, in March 2014 the Arizona Supreme Court declined to review an appeals-court decision upholding the state's ESA law. The court distinguished the ESAs from vouchers because the latter "set aside state money to allow students to attend private schools" whereas under the ESA law, "the state deposits funds into an account from which parents may draw to purchase a wide range of services" and "none of the ESA funds are pre-ordained for a particular destination."[119]

It is not clear whether Colorado courts would make the same distinction as courts in Arizona made. The fact, however, that such a distinction has been made by the top court of another state does give hope that the same could happen in Colorado.

The Bottom Line

Regardless of the legal obstacles, the goal of policymakers should be to make school-choice tools available to all parents. Giving all parents, regardless of their income level, the opportunity to choose the best education for their children makes sense because many middle-class parents, struggling from paycheck to paycheck to make ends meet, don't have the resources to afford private-school tuition or tutoring services. Also, as this study has shown, many Colorado public schools are failing to raise the performance of middle-class students.

The bottom line is that a significant number of public schools in Colorado and other states that serve middle-class students are not as good as people think they are. It is therefore critical that states enact programs, such as Nevada's groundbreaking education savings accounts, that give all parents the ability to choose the best educational options for their children. Choice is a right for all, not just for some.

Endnotes

1. Tess Stovall and Deidre Dolan, "Incomplete: How Middle Class Schools Aren't Making the Grade," Third Way, p. 2, available at: http://content.thirdway.org/publications/435/Third_Way_Report_-_Incomplete_How_Middle_Class_Schools_Aren_t_Making_the_Grade_-_PRINT.pdf

2. Tess Stovall and Deidre Dolan, p. 16.

3. Some may argue that one year of low student achievement at a school is not enough to brand the school as underperforming in general. However, research has shown that just one year of inadequate learning at a school, due, for example, to bad teaching, can have serious lasting consequences for a student. Eric Hanushek, a senior fellow at the Hoover Institution at Stanford University and one of the nation's top education economists, has researched extensively the connection between poor teaching and student performance and concludes:

   > Let's say in elementary school, you have one bad teacher. It's 1/12th of a student's education. If at some point you get a bad teacher, that puts you back, and a few bad teachers can put you quite a way's back—so much so that you might have trouble catching up. The difference between a good and a bad teacher is one year of learning in an academic year. A good teacher can get 1.5 years of learning growth; a bad teacher gets .5 years of learning growth. If you get a few bad teachers in a row, a student's life is altered dramatically.

   Potentially losing a year's learning growth is very significant, which is why this study uses one year of poor student performance at a school as the benchmark for school underperformance. See "Students First – Why an effective teacher matters: A Q&A with Eric Hanushek," Stanford University, February 8, 2011, available at http://hanushek.stanford.edu/opinions/students-first-why-effective-teacher-matters-q-eric-hanushek

4. This study uses the term "regular public schools," which excludes charter schools, alternative schools, or other non-traditional public schools. Also, this study does not use linear-regression modeling, which previous studies in the "Not as Good as You Think" series used. Linear-regression modeling estimates whether a relationship exists between the percentage of students in a school who are classified as coming from low-income households and the percent of students proficient (at grade level) in the school for a particular grade and subject. Due to data restrictions employed by Colorado, it was impossible to obtain the specific data necessary to use linear-regression modeling satisfactorily for this study.

5. The Colorado Department of Education defines economically disadvantaged as "students eligible to receive free or reduced cost lunches." See http://www.cde.state.co.us/fedprograms/dper/ayp-glossary

6   Tess Stovall and Deidre Dolan, p. 11.

7   "How Results are Reported," U.S. Department of Education, Institute of Education Sciences, National Center for Education Statistics, National Assessment of Progress, October 8, 2010. Available at: http://nces.ed.gov/nationsreportcard/about/nathowreport.asp

8   Paul Peterson and Fredrick Hess, "Few States Set World-Class Standards," *Education Next*, Summer 2008, Vol. 8, No. 3, available at: http://educationnext.org/few-states-set-worldclass-standards/

9   See "Frequently Asked Questions About NAEP Sampling," available at: http://edsource.org//wp-content/uploads/NAEP_Sampling_Frequently_Asked_Questions.pdf

10 See http://nces.ed.gov/nationsreportcard/subject/publications/stt2013/pdf/2014464CO4.pdf

11 See https://nces.ed.gov/nationsreportcard/subject/publications/stt2013/pdf/2014465CO4.pdf

12 See http://nces.ed.gov/nationsreportcard/subject/publications/stt2013/pdf/2014464CO8.pdf

13 See https://nces.ed.gov/nationsreportcard/subject/publications/stt2013/pdf/2014465CO8.pdf

14 "How Results are Reported," available at: http://nces.ed.gov/nationsreportcard/about/nathowreport.asp

15 See http://nces.ed.gov/nationsreportcard/subject/publications/stt2013/pdf/2014464CO4.pdf and https://nces.ed.gov/nationsreportcard/subject/publications/stt2013/pdf/2014465CO4.pdf

16 See http://nces.ed.gov/nationsreportcard/subject/publications/stt2013/pdf/2014464CO8.pdf

17 See https://nces.ed.gov/nationsreportcard/subject/publications/stt2013/pdf/2014465CO8.pdf

18 See http://nces.ed.gov/nationsreportcard/subject/publications/stt2013/pdf/2014465MA4.pdf

19 See http://nces.ed.gov/nationsreportcard/subject/publications/stt2013/pdf/2014464MA4.pdf

20 See http://nces.ed.gov/nationsreportcard/subject/publications/stt2013/pdf/2014465MA8.pdf

21 See http://nces.ed.gov/nationsreportcard/subject/publications/stt2013/pdf/2014464MA8.pdf

22 See https://nces.ed.gov/nationsreportcard/subject/publications/stt2013/pdf/2014465KS4.pdf

23 See http://nces.ed.gov/nationsreportcard/subject/publications/stt2013/pdf/2014464KS4.pdf

24 See http://nces.ed.gov/nationsreportcard/subject/publications/stt2013/pdf/2014465KS8.pdf

25 See https://nces.ed.gov/nationsreportcard/subject/publications/stt2013/pdf/2014464KS8.pdf

26 Lance Izumi and Alicia Chang, "Not as Good as You Think: Why Middle-Class Parents in Michigan Should be Concerned About Their Local Public Schools," Pacific Research Institute, March 2015, p. 3, available at http://www.pacificresearch.org/fileadmin/images/Studies_2015/NAGAYT_Michigan_Fweb.pdf

27 Sheila Byrd Carmichael, Gabrielle Martino, Kathleen Porter-Magee and W. Stephen Wilson, "The State of State Standards – and the Common Core – in 2010," Fordham Institute, July 2010, p. 64, available at http://www.edexcellence.net/sites/default/files/publication/pdfs/SOSSand-CC2010_FullReportFINAL_8.pdf

28 Sheila Byrd Carmichael, Gabrielle Martino, Kathleen Porter-Magee and W. Stephen Wilson, p. 66.

29 Sheila Byrd Carmichael, Gabrielle Martino, Kathleen Porter-Magee and W. Stephen Wilson, p. 67.

30 Sheila Byrd Carmichael, Gabrielle Martino, Kathleen Porter-Magee and W. Stephen Wilson, pp. 68-69.

31 While the Fordham Institute has been a vocal proponent of the Common Core national education standards, the authors would like to emphasize that Fordham is being cited for its content analysis of standards, not its position on Common Core.

32 It should be pointed out that the Colorado Department of Education boasts that it convened a broad-based stakeholder committee in May 2008 to advise the department on the development process and content of the Colorado Assessment Standards (CAS). The stakeholder committee meetings were publicized in advance and open to the public, with detailed minutes of the meetings posted on the department's website. According to the department: "Coloradans received an open invitation to participate in the standards revision process which yielded more than 700 applications from eligible candidates in K-12, early childhood and higher education, fields of business and military, librarians, and parents. 250 citizens were selected through a name-blind process to participate on ten content specific subcommittees." Then, "CDE conducted five series of public meetings in 10-13 Colorado cities between 2008 and 2010 to engage the public in providing input on the process and content of Colorado's new standards. In the first series, Coloradans had the opportunity to provide input on a variety of elements in the standards, including but not limited to, 21st century skills and the descriptions of postsecondary and workforce readiness and school readiness. Three more public feedback tours were conducted to focus on specific content areas. The fifth series was designed to solicit teacher input regarding the imple-

mentation of the new Colorado Academic Standards." The department goes on to explain: "The standards writing process began with an analysis of old Colorado standards compared to national and international benchmarks and educational research appropriate for each content area. . . . Reference of the benchmarking states and nations used as well as other resources and research can be found within the introduction of each of the Colorado Academic Standards documents." Next, "Using the research provided, over 250 Colorado education and business professionals and parents participated on standards development subcommittees to write Colorado's new academic standards. The names of the subcommittee members are also included in the standards documents." Finally, "Drafts of each set of standards were disseminated to the Colorado public and national content experts for review. In addition to public feedback gathered through feedback meetings held throughout the state, individuals could provide line-by-line recommendations on each draft through an online feedback system. After this review process, subcommittees made final revisions and the revised drafts were presented to the State Board of Education for adoption on December 10, 2009." In contrast, there was little public input into Colorado's hasty adoption of the Common Core national education standards, which were eventually incorporated into the CAS. The final Common Core standards were published in June 2010, and the Colorado State Board of Education voted to adopt them on August 2, 2010. The Board dispensed with the massive, lengthy, in-depth and open outreach to the public that marked the creation, development and adoption of the CAS from May 2008 to December 2009, and rushed through the adoption of the Common Core standards in a matter of a few weeks in the summer of 2010. By the end of 2010, the CDE released a new version of the CAS, which now included the entirety of the Common Core standards. For a full history of the development and adoption process for the CAS and the Common Core, see more at: http://www.cde.state.co.us/standardsandinstruction/cas-historyanddevelopment#sthash.u4ZyysFM.a2GlE4eH.dpuf

33 See https://www.cde.state.co.us/assessment/coassess-about

34 See https://www.cde.state.co.us/sites/default/files/documents/assessment/documents/pld achievement_level_overview.pdf

35 "Proficient vs. Prepared: Disparities Between State Tests and the 2013 National Assessment of Educational Progress (NAEP)," Achieve, May 4, 2015, available at http://www.achieve.org/files/NAEPBriefFINAL051415.pdf

36 "Proficient vs. Prepared: Disparities Between State Tests and the 2013 National Assessment of Educational Progress (NAEP)," available at http://www.achieve.org/files/NAEPBriefFINAL051415.pdf

37 "Proficient vs. Prepared: Disparities Between State Tests and the 2013 National Assessment of Educational Progress (NAEP)," available at http://www.achieve.org/files/NAEPBriefFINAL051415.pdf

38   See http://www.schoolview.org/GMFAQ.asp

39   See http://www.city-data.com/city/Thornton-Colorado.html

40   See http://www.schooldigger.com/go/CO/schools/0690001491/school.aspx

41   See http://www.city-data.com/city/Strasburg-Colorado.html. For this study, "median home value" is the median home and condominium value. For descriptive purposes, the median house/condo information used in the text of this study, unless otherwise noted, is based on the median house/condo price for the village, town or city in which the school is located. In the appendix of this study the median house/condo information in the spreadsheet for all predominantly non-low-income schools is based on the median house/condo price for the zip code in which the school is located.

42   See http://www.schooldigger.com/go/CO/schools/0675001160/school.aspx

43   See http://www.schooldigger.com/go/CO/schools/0675001161/school.aspx

44   See http://www.schooldigger.com/go/CO/schools/0291001951/school.aspx

45   See http://www.city-data.com/city/Centennial-Colorado.html

46   See http://www.centennialco.gov

47   See http://www.schooldigger.com/go/CO/schools/0291006156/school.aspx

48   See http://www.greatschools.org/colorado/centennial/275-Eaglecrest-High-School/reviews/

49   See http://www.city-data.com/city/Louisville-Colorado.html

50   See http://www.schooldigger.com/go/CO/schools/0249001632/school.aspx

51   See http://www.city-data.com/city/Longmont-Colorado.html

52   See http://www.schooldigger.com/go/CO/schools/0537001814/school.aspx

53   See http://www.city-data.com/city/Broomfield-Colorado.html

54   See http://www.schooldigger.com/go/CO/schools/0249000103/school.aspx

55   See http://www.city-data.com/city/Castle-Rock-Colorado.html

56   See http://www.schooldigger.com/go/CO/schools/0345001918/school.aspx

57 See http://www.greatschools.org/colorado/castle-rock/2499-Castle-View-High-School/reviews/

58 See http://www.greatschools.org/colorado/castle-rock/2499-Castle-View-High-School/reviews/

59 See http://www.schooldigger.com/go/CO/schools/0345000440/school.aspx

60 See http://www.greatschools.org/colorado/castle-rock/537-Douglas-County-High-School/reviews/

61 See http://www.city-data.com/city/Parker-Colorado.html

62 See http://www.schooldigger.com/go/CO/schools/0345001578/school.aspx

63 See http://www.city-data.com/city/Highlands-Ranch-Colorado.html

64 See http://www.schooldigger.com/go/CO/schools/0345001748/school.aspx

65 See http://www.city-data.com/city/Highlands-Ranch-Colorado.html

66 See http://www.schooldigger.com/go/CO/schools/0192001429/school.aspx

67 See http://www.schooldigger.com/go/CO/schools/0192001645/school.aspx

68 See http://www.greatschools.org/colorado/colorado-springs/29-Pine-Creek-High-School/reviews/

69 See http://www.schooldigger.com/go/CO/schools/0192001321/school.aspx

70 See http://www.schooldigger.com/go/CO/schools/0387006408/school.aspx

71 See http://www.greatschools.org/colorado/colorado-springs/4087-Vista-Ridge-High-School/reviews/

72 See http://www.city-data.com/city/Manitou-Springs-Colorado.html

73 See http://www.schooldigger.com/go/CO/schools/0549000946/school.aspx

74 See http://www.city-data.com/city/Elizabeth-Colorado.html

75 See http://www.schooldigger.com/go/CO/schools/0372000483/school.aspx

76 See http://www.greatschools.org/colorado/elizabeth/625-Elizabeth-High-School/reviews/

77 See http://www.city-data.com/city/Lakewood-Colorado.html

78 See http://www.schooldigger.com/go/CO/schools/0480000736/school.aspx

79 See http://www.schooldigger.com/go/CO/schools/0480000733/school.aspx

80 See http://www.schooldigger.com/go/CO/schools/0480001487/school.aspx

81 See http://www.city-data.com/city/Durango-Colorado.html

82 See http://www.schooldigger.com/go/CO/schools/0348000448/school.aspx

83 See http://www.greatschools.org/colorado/durango/581-Durango-High-School/reviews/

84 See http://www.schooldigger.com/go/CO/schools/0348000452/school.aspx

85 See http://www.city-data.com/city/Berthoud-Colorado.html

86 See http://www.schooldigger.com/go/CO/schools/0540000927/school.aspx

87 See http://www.greatschools.org/colorado/berthoud/1163-Berthoud-High-School/reviews/

88 See http://www.city-data.com/city/Loveland-Colorado.html

89 See http://www.schooldigger.com/go/CO/schools/0540000938/school.aspx

90 See http://www.greatschools.org/colorado/loveland/1174-Thompson-Valley-High-School/reviews/

91 "Best Places to Live 2006," *Money*, July 2006, see http://money.cnn.com/popups/2006/money-mag/bplive_2006/frameset.1.1.exclude.html

92 See http://www.schooldigger.com/go/CO/schools/0399000545/school.aspx

93 See http://www.schooldigger.com/go/CO/schools/0399000528/school.aspx

94 See http://www.city-data.com/city/Rangely-Colorado.html

95 See http://www.schooldigger.com/go/CO/schools/0618001086/school.aspx

96   See http://www.city-data.com/city/Highlands-Ranch-Colorado.html

97   See http://www.schooldigger.com/go/CO/schools/0687001171/school.aspx

98   See http://www.city-data.com/city/Highlands-Ranch-Colorado.html

99   See http://www.schooldigger.com/go/CO/schools/0681001164/school.aspx

100 See http://www.city-data.com/city/Windsor-Colorado.html

101 See http://www.schooldigger.com/go/CO/schools/0735001264/school.aspx

102 Elizabeth Warren and Amelia Warren Tyagi, quoted in Carrie Lukas, "Want to Help the Middle Class? Embrace School Choice," Townhall.com, October 12, 2006, available at: http://townhall.com/columnists/CarrieLukas/2006/10/12/want_to_help_the_middle_class_embrace_school_choice.

103 Elizabeth Warren and Amelia Warren Tyagi, quoted in Lewis M. Andrews, "Benefits of Choice Go Beyond Schools and into Economy," *Investor's Business Daily*, June 7, 2004.

104 Toby Young, "Cameron is right about middle-class schools 'coasting,'" *Daily Telegraph*, November 14, 2011, available at: http://blogs.telegraph.co.uk/news/tobyyoung/100117419/cameron-is-right-about-middle-class-schools-coasting-the-solution-is-to-allow-free-schools-to-be-set-up-in-affluent-r/

105 Toby Young, "Cameron is right about middle-class schools 'coasting,'" available at: http://blogs.telegraph.co.uk/news/tobyyoung/100117419/cameron-is-right-about-middle-class-schools-coasting-the-solution-is-to-allow-free-schools-to-be-set-up-in-affluent-r/

106 Elizabeth Warren and Amelia Warren Tyagi, quoted in Carrie Lukas, "Want to Help the Middle Class? Embrace School Choice," Townhall.com, October 12, 2006, available at: http://townhall.com/columnists/CarrieLukas/2006/10/12/want_to_help_the_middle_class_embrace_school_choice.

107 Jill Lepore, "The Warren Brief," *The New Yorker*, April 21, 2014, available at http://www.newyorker.com/magazine/2014/04/21/the-warren-brief

108 See http://www.schoolchoiceforkids.org/english.php?ID=6#.VbkuAs6GufQ

109 Jason Bedrick and Lindsey Burke, "The Next Step in School Choice," *National Affairs*, Winter 2015, available at http://www.nationalaffairs.com/publications/detail/the-next-step-in-school-choice

110 "ABCs of School Choice," The Friedman Foundation for Educational Choices, 2014 edition, p. 33.

111 "ABCs of School Choice," The Friedman Foundation for Educational Choices, 2014 edition, p. 33.

112 Benjamin DeGrow, "A Scholarship Tax Program for Colorado," Independence Institute, December 2014, pp. 1-2, available at http://education.i2i.org/wp-content/uploads/2015/01/IP_2_2014_revised_web_c.pdf

113 Benjamin DeGrow, "A Scholarship Tax Program for Colorado," Independence Institute, December 2014, p. 6, available at http://education.i2i.org/wp-content/uploads/2015/01/IP_2_2014_revised_web_c.pdf

114 Benjamin DeGrow, "A Scholarship Tax Program for Colorado," Independence Institute, December 2014, p. 6, available at http://education.i2i.org/wp-content/uploads/2015/01/IP_2_2014_revised_web_c.pdf

115 "The ABCs of School Choice," The Friedman Foundation for Educational Choice, 2015 edition, p. 3, available at http://www.edchoice.org/School-Choice/The-ABCs-of-School-Choice/2015-ABCs-of-School-Choice-WEB

116 Jason Bedrick and Lindsey Burke, available at http://www.nationalaffairs.com/publications/detail/the-next-step-in-school-choice

117 According to the Friedman Foundation for Educational Choice, the following are the main regulations that the Nevada ESA program imposes:
- Existing licensed or exempt private schools are allowed to participate. Distance learning programs that are not offered by the public school, a tutor or tutoring agency, a university, state college or community college within the Nevada system of Higher Education, or a parent who has submitted an application to the state treasurer are also allowed to participate. The treasurer may request additional information to demonstrate that each may serve as a participating entity. The treasurer will establish those rules. From there, each entity can be approved or denied by the treasurer.
- If any entity receives more than $50,000 in ESA funds during any school year, the entity must post a surety bond equal to the amount received, or it must demonstrate to the treasurer the ability to pay with unencumbered funds. Receipts must be given for payment for all services rendered to the child.
- No entity will be allowed to refund or rebate any payment back to a parent.
- All children must complete a nationally norm-referenced test yearly in mathematics and English and report the results to the Nevada Department of Education (DOE). The DOE will then aggregate the data according to grade level, gender, race, and family income level. After three years, the DOE will report ESA student graduation rates.

- The treasurer may refuse to allow any entity to continue to participate in the program if they determine that the entity has failed to comply with any provision of the legislation.
- The treasurer's office will make a list of participating entities annually. Additionally, the treasurer will be allowed to freeze or dissolve any accounts for noncompliance by any parent and may give notice for any account of fraud to the Attorney General or district attorney.
- Unless otherwise stated in the legislation, nothing in the legislation will be deemed to limit the independence or autonomy of any participating entity.
- The treasurer shall adopt any regulations necessary to carry out provisions of this act.
- All Nevada public school students who have been enrolled for at least 100 days prior are eligible to receive an ESA. That translates to roughly 93 percent of all Nevada school-aged children or 453,024 K–12 students. Children who received an ESA in the previous year are allowed continuing eligibility. Private and homeschool students are not eligible for the program.

See Michael Chartier, "Everything You Wanted to Know About Nevada's Universal ESA Bill," The Friedman Foundation for Educational Choice, May 29, 2015, available at http://www.edchoice.org/Blog/May-2015/Everything-You-Need-to-Know-About-Nevada-s-Univers

118 Glenn Cook, "Nevada leaps forward nationally with education savings accounts," *Las Vegas Review-Journal*, June 7, 2015, available at http://www.reviewjournal.com/columns-blogs/glenn-cook/nevada-leaps-forward-nationally-education-savings-accounts

119 Jason Bedrick and Lindsey Burke, "The Next Step in School Choice," *National Affairs*, Winter 2015, available at http://www.nationalaffairs.com/publications/detail/the-next-step-in-school-choice

Appendix
School Performance

HOW TO READ THE TABLES

% Low-Income
The percentage of economically disadvantaged students in the school. The study only includes schools in which 33 percent or fewer of the students qualify for the National School Lunch Program (NSLP).

ELA Prof. < 50%/Math Prof. < 50%
The number of grades in the school in which 50 percent or less of students scored proficient (Level 3-Proficient) on the Transitional Colorado Assessment Program (TCAP) in English language arts/reading or math in 2014.

ELA % Prof./Math % Prof.
The percentage of students that scored proficient (Level 3-Proficient) or above on the TCAP in English language arts/reading or math in 2014.

Median Home Value
The median home value in the zip code in which the school is located.

Red Bar Indicates Schools that have One or More Grades with Proficiency Rates of 50% or Less on the 2014 TCAP.

School Name	District Name	County Name	Zip Code	Median Home Value (k)	School Level
Mountain View Elementary School	Adams 12 Five Star Schools	Adams	80020	280800	1-Primary
Westlake Middle School	Adams 12 Five Star Schools	Adams	80020	280800	2-Middle
Coyote Ridge Elementary School	Adams 12 Five Star Schools	Adams	80023	508400	1-Primary
Legacy High School	Adams 12 Five Star Schools	Adams	80023	508400	3-High
Meridian Elementary School	Adams 12 Five Star Schools	Adams	80023	508400	1-Primary
Cotton Creek Elementary School	Adams 12 Five Star Schools	Adams	80031	254100	1-Primary
Hulstrom Options K-8 School	Adams 12 Five Star Schools	Adams	80233	227100	1-Primary
Stem Lab	Adams 12 Five Star Schools	Adams	80233	227100	1-Primary
Mountain Range High School	Adams 12 Five Star Schools	Adams	80234	270400	3-High
Eagleview Elementary School	Adams 12 Five Star Schools	Adams	80241	277800	1-Primary
Hunters Glen Elementary School	Adams 12 Five Star Schools	Adams	80241	277800	1-Primary
Tarver Elementary School	Adams 12 Five Star Schools	Adams	80241	277800	1-Primary
Century Middle School	Adams 12 Five Star Schools	Adams	80421	239000	2-Middle
Glacier Peak Elementary School	Adams 12 Five Star Schools	Adams	80602	356800	1-Primary
Horizon High School	Adams 12 Five Star Schools	Adams	80602	356800	3-High
Prairie Hills Elementary School	Adams 12 Five Star Schools	Adams	80602	356800	1-Primary
Rocky Top Middle School	Adams 12 Five Star Schools	Adams	80602	356800	2-Middle
Silver Creek Elementary	Adams 12 Five Star Schools	Adams	80602	356800	1-Primary
Bennett High School	Bennett 29j	Adams	80102	196700	3-High
Second Creek Elementary School	Brighton 27j	Adams	80022	195200	1-Primary
Turnberry Elementary	Brighton 27j	Adams	80022	195200	1-Primary
Brighton High School	Brighton 27j	Adams	80601	239300	3-High
West Ridge Elementary	Brighton 27j	Adams	80602	356800	1-Primary
John W Thimmig Elementary School	Brighton 27j	Adams	80640	273100	1-Primary

	Pct Soc Dis	ELA Prof < 50%	Math Prof < 50%	Grade 3		Grade 4	
				ELA Pct Prof	Math Pct Prof	ELA Pct Prof	Math Pct Prof
	26.2	0	0	80.0	81.1	70.7	80.8
	26.9	0	0	0.0	0.0	0.0	0.0
	3.0	0	0	88.5	89.8	84.8	92.2
	18.2	0	0	0.0	0.0	0.0	0.0
	5.1	0	0	84.8	87.3	85.7	89.8
	21.8	0	0	79.7	82.3	83.9	87.6
	8.1	0	0	100.0	100.0	96.8	96.8
	18.0	0	0	79.6	84.0	61.5	88.5
	29.4	0	2	0.0	0.0	0.0	0.0
	22.5	0	0	70.6	75.5	79.0	85.0
	24.3	0	0	78.2	80.7	73.9	80.7
	18.7	0	0	70.4	73.2	77.6	85.5
	30.1	0	0	0.0	0.0	0.0	0.0
	32.0	0	0	76.9	75.8	67.0	80.8
	18.3	0	2	0.0	0.0	0.0	0.0
	12.4	0	0	75.0	85.7	74.4	87.8
	14.6	0	0	0.0	0.0	0.0	0.0
	6.9	0	0	80.3	85.2	84.5	87.8
	30.7	0	2	0.0	0.0	0.0	0.0
	30.0	0	0	66.7	80.9	74.7	73.6
	24.3	0	0	78.9	79.3	76.8	75.0
	20.8	0	2	0.0	0.0	0.0	0.0
	20.0	0	0	81.1	82.0	72.6	74.3
	32.5	0	0	72.3	72.5	73.7	66.1

	Grade 5		Grade 6	
School Name	ELA Pct Prof	Math Pct Prof	ELA Pct Prof	Math Pct Prof
Mountain View Elementary School	80.2	78.5	0.0	0.0
Westlake Middle School	0.0	0.0	79.5	79.5
Coyote Ridge Elementary School	91.4	87.7	0.0	0.0
Legacy High School	0.0	0.0	0.0	0.0
Meridian Elementary School	89.1	91.4	0.0	0.0
Cotton Creek Elementary School	74.0	79.2	0.0	0.0
Hulstrom Options K-8 School	97.1	98.1	92.0	96.6
Stem Lab	85.2	90.7	84.3	78.4
Mountain Range High School	0.0	0.0	0.0	0.0
Eagleview Elementary School	80.3	81.7	0.0	0.0
Hunters Glen Elementary School	80.0	82.7	0.0	0.0
Tarver Elementary School	73.6	74.7	0.0	0.0
Century Middle School	0.0	0.0	70.3	67.2
Glacier Peak Elementary School	69.9	63.0	0.0	0.0
Horizon High School	0.0	0.0	0.0	0.0
Prairie Hills Elementary School	74.0	76.0	0.0	0.0
Rocky Top Middle School	0.0	0.0	81.1	75.4
Silver Creek Elementary	90.7	86.0	0.0	0.0
Bennett High School	0.0	0.0	0.0	0.0
Second Creek Elementary School	69.5	63.8	0.0	0.0
Turnberry Elementary	79.7	76.6	0.0	0.0
Brighton High School	0.0	0.0	0.0	0.0
West Ridge Elementary	87.1	77.4	0.0	0.0
John W Thimmig Elementary School	66.1	65.2	0.0	0.0

Grade 7		Grade 8		Grade 9		Grade 10	
ELA Pct Prof	Math Pct Prof	ELA Pct Prof	Math Pct Prof	ELA Pct Prof	Math Pct Prof	ELA Pct Prof	Math Pct Prof
0.0	0.0	0.0	0.0	0.0	0.0	0.0	0.0
76.4	75.4	76.5	65.7	0.0	0.0	0.0	0.0
0.0	0.0	0.0	0.0	0.0	0.0	0.0	0.0
0.0	0.0	0.0	0.0	81.0	62.1	81.3	54.7
0.0	0.0	0.0	0.0	0.0	0.0	0.0	0.0
0.0	0.0	0.0	0.0	0.0	0.0	0.0	0.0
92.5	94.0	94.3	91.4	0.0	0.0	0.0	0.0
90.4	73.1	88.0	76.0	0.0	0.0	0.0	0.0
0.0	0.0	0.0	0.0	69.3	39.4	73.8	33.1
0.0	0.0	0.0	0.0	0.0	0.0	0.0	0.0
0.0	0.0	0.0	0.0	0.0	0.0	0.0	0.0
0.0	0.0	0.0	0.0	0.0	0.0	0.0	0.0
74.1	62.4	72.3	56.0	0.0	0.0	0.0	0.0
0.0	0.0	0.0	0.0	0.0	0.0	0.0	0.0
0.0	0.0	0.0	0.0	63.1	46.9	72.1	39.5
0.0	0.0	0.0	0.0	0.0	0.0	0.0	0.0
73.4	71.1	76.9	66.5	0.0	0.0	0.0	0.0
0.0	0.0	0.0	0.0	0.0	0.0	0.0	0.0
0.0	0.0	0.0	0.0	58.9	26.7	62.7	23.9
0.0	0.0	0.0	0.0	0.0	0.0	0.0	0.0
0.0	0.0	0.0	0.0	0.0	0.0	0.0	0.0
0.0	0.0	0.0	0.0	60.0	24.9	64.5	21.3
0.0	0.0	0.0	0.0	0.0	0.0	0.0	0.0
0.0	0.0	0.0	0.0	0.0	0.0	0.0	0.0

School Name	District Name	County Name	Zip Code	Median Home Value (k)	School Level
Prairie View High School	Brighton 27j	Adams	80640	273100	3-High
Hemphill Middle School	Strasburg 31j	Adams	80136	233800	2-Middle
Strasburg Elementary School	Strasburg 31j	Adams	80136	233800	1-Primary
Strasburg High School	Strasburg 31j	Adams	80136	233800	3-High
Aurora Quest K-8	Adams-Arapahoe 28j	Arapahoe	80011	183000	1-Primary
Aurora Frontier K-8	Adams-Arapahoe 28j	Arapahoe	80013	238800	1-Primary
Murphy Creek K-8 School	Adams-Arapahoe 28j	Arapahoe	80018	305100	1-Primary
Dakota Valley Elementary School	Cherry Creek 5	Arapahoe	80013	238800	1-Primary
Antelope Ridge Elementary School	Cherry Creek 5	Arapahoe	80015	294500	1-Primary
Aspen Crossing Elementary School	Cherry Creek 5	Arapahoe	80015	294500	1-Primary
Canyon Creek Elementary School	Cherry Creek 5	Arapahoe	80015	294500	1-Primary
Eaglecrest High School	Cherry Creek 5	Arapahoe	80015	294500	3-High
Indian Ridge Elementary School	Cherry Creek 5	Arapahoe	80015	294500	1-Primary
Peakview Elementary School	Cherry Creek 5	Arapahoe	80015	294500	1-Primary
Rolling Hills Elementary School	Cherry Creek 5	Arapahoe	80015	294500	1-Primary
Sagebrush Elementary School	Cherry Creek 5	Arapahoe	80015	294500	1-Primary
Sky Vista Middle School	Cherry Creek 5	Arapahoe	80015	294500	2-Middle
Smoky Hill High School	Cherry Creek 5	Arapahoe	80015	294500	3-High
Thunder Ridge Middle School	Cherry Creek 5	Arapahoe	80015	294500	2-Middle
Timberline Elementary School	Cherry Creek 5	Arapahoe	80015	294500	1-Primary
Trails West Elementary School	Cherry Creek 5	Arapahoe	80015	294500	1-Primary
Buffalo Trail Elementary School	Cherry Creek 5	Arapahoe	80016	434300	1-Primary
Cherokee Trail High School	Cherry Creek 5	Arapahoe	80016	434300	3-High
Coyote Hills Elementary School	Cherry Creek 5	Arapahoe	80016	434300	1-Primary
Creekside Elementary School	Cherry Creek 5	Arapahoe	80016	434300	1-Primary
Falcon Creek Middle School	Cherry Creek 5	Arapahoe	80016	434300	2-Middle
Fox Hollow Elementary School	Cherry Creek 5	Arapahoe	80016	434300	1-Primary
Fox Ridge Middle School	Cherry Creek 5	Arapahoe	80016	434300	2-Middle
Grandview High School	Cherry Creek 5	Arapahoe	80016	434300	3-High
Liberty Middle School	Cherry Creek 5	Arapahoe	80016	434300	2-Middle
Pine Ridge Elementary School	Cherry Creek 5	Arapahoe	80016	434300	1-Primary
Cherry Hills Village Elementary School	Cherry Creek 5	Arapahoe	80110	246600	1-Primary
Belleview Elementary School	Cherry Creek 5	Arapahoe	80111	508000	1-Primary

Pct Soc Dis	ELA Prof < 50%	Math Prof < 50%	Grade 3		Grade 4	
			ELA Pct Prof	Math Pct Prof	ELA Pct Prof	Math Pct Prof
32.7	0	2	0.0	0.0	0.0	0.0
23.4	0	2	0.0	0.0	0.0	0.0
25.9	0	0	61.8	73.2	89.1	87.5
13.4	0	2	0.0	0.0	0.0	0.0
23.2	0	0	96.4	98.2	100.0	100.0
30.7	0	1	83.3	72.7	78.4	74.3
32.2	0	1	73.1	67.7	63.6	71.2
17.2	0	0	78.7	73.2	72.0	78.8
17.3	0	0	78.8	78.8	85.2	88.3
13.8	0	0	78.0	89.1	83.7	88.8
19.3	0	0	80.7	81.0	81.2	86.1
26.0	0	2	0.0	0.0	0.0	0.0
8.2	0	0	83.1	89.6	78.7	92.1
17.0	0	0	87.0	79.8	78.1	87.4
7.6	0	0	94.1	94.2	83.6	86.5
31.9	0	0	63.2	63.5	60.8	67.1
21.1	0	0	0.0	0.0	0.0	0.0
27.1	0	2	0.0	0.0	0.0	0.0
19.3	0	0	0.0	0.0	0.0	0.0
16.2	0	0	80.2	84.4	74.5	81.3
21.5	0	0	85.2	81.9	64.6	68.8
15.0	0	0	77.0	82.0	76.7	81.7
12.9	0	1	0.0	0.0	0.0	0.0
5.2	0	0	88.8	94.4	94.3	92.7
13.1	0	0	77.6	84.2	90.1	89.4
24.4	0	0	0.0	0.0	0.0	0.0
8.7	0	0	82.6	89.2	87.2	88.9
10.4	0	0	0.0	0.0	0.0	0.0
16.1	0	0	0.0	0.0	0.0	0.0
20.2	0	0	0.0	0.0	0.0	0.0
6.1	0	0	90.9	89.5	81.5	89.0
2.6	0	0	92.2	93.2	99.1	97.3
11.3	0	0	82.8	88.6	88.0	97.0

School Name	Grade 5		Grade 6	
	ELA Pct Prof	Math Pct Prof	ELA Pct Prof	Math Pct Prof
Prairie View High School	0.0	0.0	0.0	0.0
Hemphill Middle School	0.0	0.0	75.3	53.8
Strasburg Elementary School	65.8	56.6	0.0	0.0
Strasburg High School	0.0	0.0	0.0	0.0
Aurora Quest K-8	100.0	100.0	100.0	98.8
Aurora Frontier K-8	69.4	61.2	70.1	72.7
Murphy Creek K-8 School	72.8	56.8	68.9	44.6
Dakota Valley Elementary School	81.0	69.8	0.0	0.0
Antelope Ridge Elementary School	85.2	79.4	0.0	0.0
Aspen Crossing Elementary School	82.5	81.4	0.0	0.0
Canyon Creek Elementary School	71.7	60.0	0.0	0.0
Eaglecrest High School	0.0	0.0	0.0	0.0
Indian Ridge Elementary School	86.8	81.3	0.0	0.0
Peakview Elementary School	88.8	78.5	0.0	0.0
Rolling Hills Elementary School	91.1	91.2	0.0	0.0
Sagebrush Elementary School	69.4	61.2	0.0	0.0
Sky Vista Middle School	0.0	0.0	80.6	71.4
Smoky Hill High School	0.0	0.0	0.0	0.0
Thunder Ridge Middle School	0.0	0.0	73.3	68.9
Timberline Elementary School	76.1	69.0	0.0	0.0
Trails West Elementary School	74.7	66.3	0.0	0.0
Buffalo Trail Elementary School	80.5	78.3	0.0	0.0
Cherokee Trail High School	0.0	0.0	0.0	0.0
Coyote Hills Elementary School	90.6	85.8	0.0	0.0
Creekside Elementary School	91.1	87.9	0.0	0.0
Falcon Creek Middle School	0.0	0.0	76.1	68.4
Fox Hollow Elementary School	88.8	88.8	0.0	0.0
Fox Ridge Middle School	0.0	0.0	83.7	81.4
Grandview High School	0.0	0.0	0.0	0.0
Liberty Middle School	0.0	0.0	84.3	75.0
Pine Ridge Elementary School	85.8	88.7	0.0	0.0
Cherry Hills Village Elementary School	97.1	97.1	0.0	0.0
Belleview Elementary School	92.2	90.2	0.0	0.0

Grade 7		Grade 8		Grade 9		Grade 10	
ELA Pct Prof	Math Pct Prof	ELA Pct Prof	Math Pct Prof	ELA Pct Prof	Math Pct Prof	ELA Pct Prof	Math Pct Prof
0.0	0.0	0.0	0.0	63.9	29.4	61.6	19.4
62.9	47.1	60.5	46.0	0.0	0.0	0.0	0.0
0.0	0.0	0.0	0.0	0.0	0.0	0.0	0.0
0.0	0.0	0.0	0.0	73.3	23.5	73.3	17.4
100.0	100.0	98.7	98.7	0.0	0.0	0.0	0.0
77.8	61.1	77.8	50.0	0.0	0.0	0.0	0.0
76.4	67.3	71.8	57.8	0.0	0.0	0.0	0.0
0.0	0.0	0.0	0.0	0.0	0.0	0.0	0.0
0.0	0.0	0.0	0.0	0.0	0.0	0.0	0.0
0.0	0.0	0.0	0.0	0.0	0.0	0.0	0.0
0.0	0.0	0.0	0.0	0.0	0.0	0.0	0.0
0.0	0.0	0.0	0.0	70.8	43.0	74.3	33.4
0.0	0.0	0.0	0.0	0.0	0.0	0.0	0.0
0.0	0.0	0.0	0.0	0.0	0.0	0.0	0.0
0.0	0.0	0.0	0.0	0.0	0.0	0.0	0.0
0.0	0.0	0.0	0.0	0.0	0.0	0.0	0.0
73.1	65.5	71.0	58.1	0.0	0.0	0.0	0.0
0.0	0.0	0.0	0.0	71.0	41.2	76.2	35.8
77.6	62.9	77.1	59.3	0.0	0.0	0.0	0.0
0.0	0.0	0.0	0.0	0.0	0.0	0.0	0.0
0.0	0.0	0.0	0.0	0.0	0.0	0.0	0.0
0.0	0.0	0.0	0.0	0.0	0.0	0.0	0.0
0.0	0.0	0.0	0.0	78.7	51.0	78.9	40.7
0.0	0.0	0.0	0.0	0.0	0.0	0.0	0.0
0.0	0.0	0.0	0.0	0.0	0.0	0.0	0.0
75.3	65.4	83.1	64.7	0.0	0.0	0.0	0.0
0.0	0.0	0.0	0.0	0.0	0.0	0.0	0.0
85.0	80.3	82.1	67.8	0.0	0.0	0.0	0.0
0.0	0.0	0.0	0.0	80.3	50.4	86.4	51.6
83.9	71.1	79.1	64.4	0.0	0.0	0.0	0.0
0.0	0.0	0.0	0.0	0.0	0.0	0.0	0.0
0.0	0.0	0.0	0.0	0.0	0.0	0.0	0.0
0.0	0.0	0.0	0.0	0.0	0.0	0.0	0.0

School Name	District Name	County Name	Zip Code	Median Home Value (k)	School Level
Campus Middle School	Cherry Creek 5	Arapahoe	80111	508000	2-Middle
Cherry Creek High School	Cherry Creek 5	Arapahoe	80111	508000	3-High
Cottonwood Creek Elementary School	Cherry Creek 5	Arapahoe	80111	508000	1-Primary
Greenwood Elementary School	Cherry Creek 5	Arapahoe	80111	508000	1-Primary
Heritage Elementary School	Cherry Creek 5	Arapahoe	80111	508000	1-Primary
High Plains Elementary School	Cherry Creek 5	Arapahoe	80111	508000	1-Primary
Dry Creek Elementary School	Cherry Creek 5	Arapahoe	80112	366700	1-Primary
Homestead Elementary School	Cherry Creek 5	Arapahoe	80112	366700	1-Primary
Walnut Hills Community Elementary School	Cherry Creek 5	Arapahoe	80112	366700	1-Primary
Willow Creek Elementary School	Cherry Creek 5	Arapahoe	80112	366700	1-Primary
West Middle School	Cherry Creek 5	Arapahoe	80121	355600	2-Middle
Challenge School	Cherry Creek 5	Arapahoe	80247	144100	1-Primary
Euclid Middle School	Littleton 6	Arapahoe	80120	311900	2-Middle
Heritage High School	Littleton 6	Arapahoe	80120	311900	3-High
Runyon Elementary School	Littleton 6	Arapahoe	80120	311900	1-Primary
Franklin Elementary School	Littleton 6	Arapahoe	80121	355600	1-Primary
Highland Elementary School	Littleton 6	Arapahoe	80121	355600	1-Primary
Littleton High School	Littleton 6	Arapahoe	80121	355600	3-High
Lois Lenski Elementary School	Littleton 6	Arapahoe	80121	355600	1-Primary
Peabody Elementary School	Littleton 6	Arapahoe	80121	355600	1-Primary
Arapahoe High School	Littleton 6	Arapahoe	80122	352300	3-High
Hopkins Elementary School	Littleton 6	Arapahoe	80122	352300	1-Primary
John Wesley Powell Middle School	Littleton 6	Arapahoe	80122	352300	2-Middle
Newton Middle School	Littleton 6	Arapahoe	80122	352300	2-Middle
Sandburg Elementary School	Littleton 6	Arapahoe	80122	352300	1-Primary
Twain Elementary School	Littleton 6	Arapahoe	80122	352300	1-Primary
Wilder Elementary School	Littleton 6	Arapahoe	80123	306700	1-Primary
Aspen Creek K-8 School	Boulder Valley Re 2	Boulder	80020	280800	1-Primary
Birch Elementary School	Boulder Valley Re 2	Boulder	80020	280800	1-Primary
Broomfield Heights Middle School	Boulder Valley Re 2	Boulder	80020	280800	2-Middle
Broomfield High School	Boulder Valley Re 2	Boulder	80020	280800	3-High
Kohl Elementary School	Boulder Valley Re 2	Boulder	80020	280800	1-Primary
Centaurus High School	Boulder Valley Re 2	Boulder	80026	330600	3-High
Lafayette Elementary School	Boulder Valley Re 2	Boulder	80026	330600	1-Primary

Pct Soc Dis	ELA Prof < 50%	Math Prof < 50%	Grade 3		Grade 4	
			ELA Pct Prof	Math Pct Prof	ELA Pct Prof	Math Pct Prof
13.1	0	0	0.0	0.0	0.0	0.0
9.2	0	0	0.0	0.0	0.0	0.0
4.1	0	0	90.1	90.2	92.9	98.3
4.5	0	0	91.2	90.0	97.2	95.8
7.8	0	0	91.3	93.2	97.7	97.7
18.3	0	0	86.5	93.2	87.1	86.2
11.0	0	0	89.9	88.4	94.2	88.4
5.8	0	0	96.7	96.7	96.3	93.9
16.5	0	0	80.3	82.0	81.6	86.8
4.0	0	0	95.5	94.3	90.3	96.8
12.8	0	0	0.0	0.0	0.0	0.0
5.2	0	0	98.3	96.6	100.0	100.0
29.9	0	0	0.0	0.0	0.0	0.0
14.5	0	0	0.0	0.0	0.0	0.0
10.4	0	0	81.4	81.4	89.4	92.9
10.1	0	0	94.6	93.5	92.8	91.8
20.6	0	0	86.9	75.4	80.0	85.5
25.9	0	2	0.0	0.0	0.0	0.0
6.7	0	0	99.1	93.8	96.1	96.1
20.1	0	0	80.7	82.8	72.2	84.7
6.7	0	0	0.0	0.0	0.0	0.0
21.6	0	0	79.2	77.5	83.0	83.0
10.0	0	0	0.0	0.0	0.0	0.0
18.0	0	0	0.0	0.0	0.0	0.0
9.1	0	0	91.7	90.0	92.5	90.4
19.0	0	0	85.7	87.1	77.8	79.4
6.2	0	0	95.8	99.2	91.8	94.5
12.4	0	0	85.3	82.4	82.4	82.2
32.6	0	0	73.2	75.9	61.3	79.0
29.4	0	0	0.0	0.0	0.0	0.0
13.0	0	2	0.0	0.0	0.0	0.0
19.0	0	0	80.9	75.3	76.5	82.3
29.6	0	2	0.0	0.0	0.0	0.0
22.9	0	0	83.2	76.4	76.2	78.2

School Name	Grade 5		Grade 6	
	ELA Pct Prof	Math Pct Prof	ELA Pct Prof	Math Pct Prof
Campus Middle School	0.0	0.0	89.8	90.5
Cherry Creek High School	0.0	0.0	0.0	0.0
Cottonwood Creek Elementary School	96.5	93.9	0.0	0.0
Greenwood Elementary School	94.8	93.5	0.0	0.0
Heritage Elementary School	79.1	79.1	0.0	0.0
High Plains Elementary School	92.2	86.7	0.0	0.0
Dry Creek Elementary School	94.0	92.5	0.0	0.0
Homestead Elementary School	92.7	93.8	0.0	0.0
Walnut Hills Community Elementary School	78.6	71.4	0.0	0.0
Willow Creek Elementary School	95.3	96.5	0.0	0.0
West Middle School	0.0	0.0	90.8	86.8
Challenge School	100.0	100.0	100.0	100.0
Euclid Middle School	0.0	0.0	83.5	69.1
Heritage High School	0.0	0.0	0.0	0.0
Runyon Elementary School	94.4	80.6	0.0	0.0
Franklin Elementary School	91.6	83.1	0.0	0.0
Highland Elementary School	79.1	82.1	0.0	0.0
Littleton High School	0.0	0.0	0.0	0.0
Lois Lenski Elementary School	95.6	94.7	0.0	0.0
Peabody Elementary School	82.9	80.3	0.0	0.0
Arapahoe High School	0.0	0.0	0.0	0.0
Hopkins Elementary School	85.4	75.0	0.0	0.0
John Wesley Powell Middle School	0.0	0.0	89.6	79.9
Newton Middle School	0.0	0.0	86.5	86.4
Sandburg Elementary School	91.2	87.9	0.0	0.0
Twain Elementary School	80.8	76.6	0.0	0.0
Wilder Elementary School	97.3	92.9	0.0	0.0
Aspen Creek K-8 School	81.4	76.7	89.9	78.4
Birch Elementary School	60.9	54.7	0.0	0.0
Broomfield Heights Middle School	0.0	0.0	79.5	65.5
Broomfield High School	0.0	0.0	0.0	0.0
Kohl Elementary School	78.8	74.6	0.0	0.0
Centaurus High School	0.0	0.0	0.0	0.0
Lafayette Elementary School	78.6	73.5	0.0	0.0

Grade 7		Grade 8		Grade 9		Grade 10	
ELA Pct Prof	Math Pct Prof	ELA Pct Prof	Math Pct Prof	ELA Pct Prof	Math Pct Prof	ELA Pct Prof	Math Pct Prof
87.4	80.9	88.3	84.5	0.0	0.0	0.0	0.0
0.0	0.0	0.0	0.0	87.4	74.5	85.0	67.2
0.0	0.0	0.0	0.0	0.0	0.0	0.0	0.0
0.0	0.0	0.0	0.0	0.0	0.0	0.0	0.0
0.0	0.0	0.0	0.0	0.0	0.0	0.0	0.0
0.0	0.0	0.0	0.0	0.0	0.0	0.0	0.0
0.0	0.0	0.0	0.0	0.0	0.0	0.0	0.0
0.0	0.0	0.0	0.0	0.0	0.0	0.0	0.0
0.0	0.0	0.0	0.0	0.0	0.0	0.0	0.0
0.0	0.0	0.0	0.0	0.0	0.0	0.0	0.0
89.6	86.8	87.3	75.3	0.0	0.0	0.0	0.0
98.7	98.7	100.0	98.5	0.0	0.0	0.0	0.0
81.8	70.0	79.1	64.6	0.0	0.0	0.0	0.0
0.0	0.0	0.0	0.0	81.1	59.3	85.0	55.2
0.0	0.0	0.0	0.0	0.0	0.0	0.0	0.0
0.0	0.0	0.0	0.0	0.0	0.0	0.0	0.0
0.0	0.0	0.0	0.0	0.0	0.0	0.0	0.0
0.0	0.0	0.0	0.0	69.7	43.9	73.6	42.9
0.0	0.0	0.0	0.0	0.0	0.0	0.0	0.0
0.0	0.0	0.0	0.0	0.0	0.0	0.0	0.0
0.0	0.0	0.0	0.0	86.5	62.0	88.1	53.0
0.0	0.0	0.0	0.0	0.0	0.0	0.0	0.0
87.6	83.0	92.5	78.2	0.0	0.0	0.0	0.0
82.7	81.1	80.7	83.7	0.0	0.0	0.0	0.0
0.0	0.0	0.0	0.0	0.0	0.0	0.0	0.0
0.0	0.0	0.0	0.0	0.0	74.0	85.0	0.0
0.0	0.0	0.0	0.0	0.0	0.0	0.0	0.0
80.5	66.4	78.9	60.5	0.0	0.0	0.0	0.0
0.0	0.0	0.0	0.0	0.0	0.0	0.0	0.0
80.1	62.0	76.0	53.5	0.0	0.0	0.0	0.0
0.0	0.0	0.0	0.0	71.7	45.5	78.2	43.9
0.0	0.0	0.0	0.0	0.0	0.0	0.0	0.0
0.0	0.0	0.0	0.0	70.2	46.3	69.7	35.7
0.0	0.0	0.0	0.0	0.0	0.0	0.0	0.0

School Name	District Name	County Name	Zip Code	Median Home Value (k)	School Level
Ryan Elementary School	Boulder Valley Re 2	Boulder	80026	330600	1-Primary
Coal Creek Elementary School	Boulder Valley Re 2	Boulder	80027	460100	1-Primary
Eldorado K-8 School	Boulder Valley Re 2	Boulder	80027	460100	1-Primary
Fireside Elementary School	Boulder Valley Re 2	Boulder	80027	460100	1-Primary
Louisville Elementary School	Boulder Valley Re 2	Boulder	80027	460100	1-Primary
Louisville Middle School	Boulder Valley Re 2	Boulder	80027	460100	2-Middle
Monarch High School	Boulder Valley Re 2	Boulder	80027	460100	3-High
Monarch K-8 School	Boulder Valley Re 2	Boulder	80027	460100	1-Primary
Superior Elementary School	Boulder Valley Re 2	Boulder	80027	460100	1-Primary
Heatherwood Elementary School	Boulder Valley Re 2	Boulder	80301	415200	1-Primary
Boulder High School	Boulder Valley Re 2	Boulder	80302	621200	3-High
Flatirons Elementary School	Boulder Valley Re 2	Boulder	80302	621200	1-Primary
New Vista High School	Boulder Valley Re 2	Boulder	80302	621200	3-High
Boulder Community School/Integrated Studies	Boulder Valley Re 2	Boulder	80303	505800	1-Primary
Boulder Universal	Boulder Valley Re 2	Boulder	80303	505800	4-Other
Douglass Elementary School	Boulder Valley Re 2	Boulder	80303	505800	1-Primary
Eisenhower Elementary School	Boulder Valley Re 2	Boulder	80303	505800	1-Primary
High Peaks Elementary School	Boulder Valley Re 2	Boulder	80303	505800	1-Primary
Manhattan Middle School Of The Arts And Academics	Boulder Valley Re 2	Boulder	80303	505800	2-Middle
Nevin Platt Middle School	Boulder Valley Re 2	Boulder	80303	505800	2-Middle
Centennial Middle School	Boulder Valley Re 2	Boulder	80304	685400	2-Middle
Crest View Elementary School	Boulder Valley Re 2	Boulder	80304	685400	1-Primary
Foothill Elementary School	Boulder Valley Re 2	Boulder	80304	685400	1-Primary
Bear Creek Elementary School	Boulder Valley Re 2	Boulder	80305	541600	1-Primary
Community Montessori School	Boulder Valley Re 2	Boulder	80305	541600	1-Primary
Fairview High School	Boulder Valley Re 2	Boulder	80305	541600	3-High
Mesa Elementary School	Boulder Valley Re 2	Boulder	80305	541600	1-Primary
Southern Hills Middle School	Boulder Valley Re 2	Boulder	80305	541600	2-Middle
Nederland Elementary School	Boulder Valley Re 2	Boulder	80466	341900	1-Primary
Nederland Middle-Senior High School	Boulder Valley Re 2	Boulder	80466	341900	4-Other
Fall River Elementary School	St Vrain Valley Re 1j	Boulder	80501	236600	1-Primary
St. Vrain Global Online Academy	St Vrain Valley Re 1j	Boulder	80501	236600	
Altona Middle School	St Vrain Valley Re 1j	Boulder	80503	384800	2-Middle
Blue Mountain Elementary	St Vrain Valley Re 1j	Boulder	80503	384800	1-Primary

	Pct Soc Dis	ELA Prof < 50%	Math Prof < 50%	Grade 3		Grade 4	
				ELA Pct Prof	Math Pct Prof	ELA Pct Prof	Math Pct Prof
	31.1	0	0	81.8	74.5	66.2	72.3
	9.5	0	0	87.7	87.7	81.6	89.5
	6.0	0	0	89.1	89.1	93.8	90.8
	13.7	0	0	86.8	76.5	88.9	84.2
	14.4	0	0	89.2	82.8	86.7	83.8
	12.5	0	0	0.0	0.0	0.0	0.0
	7.6	0	1	0.0	0.0	0.0	0.0
	9.8	0	0	82.3	82.7	82.7	85.7
	2.0	0	0	94.7	93.6	96.9	97.9
	11.2	0	0	92.7	94.6	95.2	91.9
	16.8	0	0	0.0	0.0	0.0	0.0
	6.3	0	0	86.0	90.0	92.5	88.7
	19.3	0	2	0.0	0.0	0.0	0.0
	17.7	0	0	90.2	86.3	89.6	89.6
	10.4	0	0	0.0	0.0	0.0	0.0
	5.5	0	0	86.1	86.1	84.7	95.3
	17.2	0	0	88.9	88.7	75.0	85.3
	10.7	0	0	93.9	89.8	98.0	100.0
	28.8	0	0	0.0	0.0	0.0	0.0
	9.8	0	0	0.0	0.0	0.0	0.0
	23.5	0	0	0.0	0.0	0.0	0.0
	21.2	0	0	83.2	84.9	75.0	78.1
	11.4	0	0	85.4	86.6	92.2	88.3
	4.3	0	0	98.6	95.9	94.4	98.2
	20.8	0	0	95.6	88.9	80.5	82.9
	7.3	0	0	0.0	0.0	0.0	0.0
	3.1	0	0	86.5	87.8	94.1	88.2
	4.4	0	0	0.0	0.0	0.0	0.0
	26.3	0	0	86.0	73.8	76.7	76.7
	23.6	0	3	0.0	0.0	0.0	0.0
	14.8	0	0	91.9	86.2	83.8	87.5
	28.4	0	1	0.0	0.0	0.0	0.0
	18.7	0	0	0.0	0.0	0.0	0.0
	7.7	0	0	92.4	95.7	90.2	91.2

	Grade 5		Grade 6	
School Name	ELA Pct Prof	Math Pct Prof	ELA Pct Prof	Math Pct Prof
Ryan Elementary School	84.7	87.5	0.0	0.0
Coal Creek Elementary School	90.1	92.6	0.0	0.0
Eldorado K-8 School	88.1	83.5	94.1	88.2
Fireside Elementary School	85.9	85.9	0.0	0.0
Louisville Elementary School	84.7	82.6	0.0	0.0
Louisville Middle School	0.0	0.0	90.5	80.5
Monarch High School	0.0	0.0	0.0	0.0
Monarch K-8 School	84.7	72.9	85.3	75.0
Superior Elementary School	93.7	90.1	0.0	0.0
Heatherwood Elementary School	85.1	83.8	0.0	0.0
Boulder High School	0.0	0.0	0.0	0.0
Flatirons Elementary School	89.3	80.4	0.0	0.0
New Vista High School	0.0	0.0	0.0	0.0
Boulder Community School/Integrated Studies	98.0	96.0	0.0	0.0
Boulder Universal	0.0	0.0	0.0	0.0
Douglass Elementary School	93.6	89.7	0.0	0.0
Eisenhower Elementary School	89.3	85.3	0.0	0.0
High Peaks Elementary School	91.7	95.9	0.0	0.0
Manhattan Middle School Of The Arts And Academics	0.0	0.0	85.2	73.0
Nevin Platt Middle School	0.0	0.0	92.4	84.9
Centennial Middle School	0.0	0.0	86.7	77.7
Crest View Elementary School	86.2	84.5	0.0	0.0
Foothill Elementary School	91.5	87.2	0.0	0.0
Bear Creek Elementary School	97.1	98.6	0.0	0.0
Community Montessori School	84.8	78.8	0.0	0.0
Fairview High School	0.0	0.0	0.0	0.0
Mesa Elementary School	95.2	93.7	0.0	0.0
Southern Hills Middle School	0.0	0.0	91.5	88.2
Nederland Elementary School	81.6	64.7	0.0	0.0
Nederland Middle-Senior High School	0.0	0.0	81.1	70.3
Fall River Elementary School	92.5	83.9	0.0	0.0
St. Vrain Global Online Academy	0.0	0.0	0.0	0.0
Altona Middle School	0.0	0.0	90.3	82.3
Blue Mountain Elementary	93.7	89.9	0.0	0.0

Grade 7		Grade 8		Grade 9		Grade 10	
ELA Pct Prof	Math Pct Prof	ELA Pct Prof	Math Pct Prof	ELA Pct Prof	Math Pct Prof	ELA Pct Prof	Math Pct Prof
0.0	0.0	0.0	0.0	0.0	0.0	0.0	0.0
0.0	0.0	0.0	0.0	0.0	0.0	0.0	0.0
90.7	76.3	90.5	81.0	0.0	0.0	0.0	0.0
0.0	0.0	0.0	0.0	0.0	0.0	0.0	0.0
0.0	0.0	0.0	0.0	0.0	0.0	0.0	0.0
88.2	77.7	88.9	74.2	0.0	0.0	0.0	0.0
0.0	0.0	0.0	0.0	82.0	61.4	76.8	49.2
88.1	78.0	88.8	79.8	0.0	0.0	0.0	0.0
0.0	0.0	0.0	0.0	0.0	0.0	0.0	0.0
0.0	0.0	0.0	0.0	0.0	0.0	0.0	0.0
0.0	0.0	0.0	0.0	80.9	55.6	76.5	51.8
0.0	0.0	0.0	0.0	0.0	0.0	0.0	0.0
0.0	0.0	0.0	0.0	82.0	46.0	80.0	28.9
0.0	0.0	0.0	0.0	0.0	0.0	0.0	0.0
0.0	0.0	0.0	0.0	0.0	0.0	76.9	57.1
0.0	0.0	0.0	0.0	0.0	0.0	0.0	0.0
0.0	0.0	0.0	0.0	0.0	0.0	0.0	0.0
0.0	0.0	0.0	0.0	0.0	0.0	0.0	0.0
78.0	63.2	70.6	63.4	0.0	0.0	0.0	0.0
88.5	83.3	84.8	68.9	0.0	0.0	0.0	0.0
71.5	56.2	77.3	66.2	0.0	0.0	0.0	0.0
0.0	0.0	0.0	0.0	0.0	0.0	0.0	0.0
0.0	0.0	0.0	0.0	0.0	0.0	0.0	0.0
0.0	0.0	0.0	0.0	0.0	0.0	0.0	0.0
0.0	0.0	0.0	0.0	0.0	0.0	0.0	0.0
0.0	0.0	0.0	0.0	90.6	77.6	89.2	73.1
0.0	0.0	0.0	0.0	0.0	0.0	0.0	0.0
95.5	93.2	91.5	83.2	0.0	0.0	0.0	0.0
0.0	0.0	0.0	0.0	0.0	0.0	0.0	0.0
80.4	52.9	61.8	38.2	51.4	25.7	79.2	25.0
0.0	0.0	0.0	0.0	0.0	0.0	0.0	0.0
0.0	0.0	0.0	0.0	0.0	0.0	90.5	14.3
88.0	81.2	89.9	83.2	0.0	0.0	0.0	0.0
0.0	0.0	0.0	0.0	0.0	0.0	0.0	0.0

School Name	District Name	County Name	Zip Code	Median Home Value (k)	School Level
Eagle Crest Elementary School	St Vrain Valley Re 1j	Boulder	80503	384800	1-Primary
Hygiene Elementary School	St Vrain Valley Re 1j	Boulder	80503	384800	1-Primary
Longmont Estates Elementary School	St Vrain Valley Re 1j	Boulder	80503	384800	1-Primary
Niwot Elementary School	St Vrain Valley Re 1j	Boulder	80503	384800	1-Primary
Niwot High School	St Vrain Valley Re 1j	Boulder	80503	384800	3-High
Silver Creek High School	St Vrain Valley Re 1j	Boulder	80503	384800	3-High
Westview Middle School	St Vrain Valley Re 1j	Boulder	80503	384800	2-Middle
Alpine Elementary School	St Vrain Valley Re 1j	Boulder	80504	304800	1-Primary
Frederick Senior High School	St Vrain Valley Re 1j	Boulder	80504	304800	3-High
Legacy Elementary School	St Vrain Valley Re 1j	Boulder	80504	304800	1-Primary
Mead High School	St Vrain Valley Re 1j	Boulder	80504	304800	4-Other
Prairie Ridge Elementary School	St Vrain Valley Re 1j	Boulder	80504	304800	1-Primary
Black Rock Elementary	St Vrain Valley Re 1j	Boulder	80516	389700	1-Primary
Erie Elementary School	St Vrain Valley Re 1j	Boulder	80516	389700	1-Primary
Erie High School	St Vrain Valley Re 1j	Boulder	80516	389700	3-High
Erie Middle School	St Vrain Valley Re 1j	Boulder	80516	389700	2-Middle
Red Hawk Elementary	St Vrain Valley Re 1j	Boulder	80516	389700	
Lyons Elementary School	St Vrain Valley Re 1j	Boulder	80540	362000	1-Primary
Lyons Middle/Senior High School	St Vrain Valley Re 1j	Boulder	80540	362000	4-Other
Mead Elementary School	St Vrain Valley Re 1j	Boulder	80542	288400	1-Primary
Mead Middle School	St Vrain Valley Re 1j	Boulder	80542	288400	2-Middle
Buena Vista High School	Buena Vista R-31	Chaffee	81211	232900	3-High
Clear Creek High School	Clear Creek Re-1	Clear Creek	80439	457000	3-High
Clear Creek Middle School	Clear Creek Re-1	Clear Creek	80439	457000	2-Middle
King-Murphy Elementary School	Clear Creek Re-1	Clear Creek	80439	457000	1-Primary
Rocky Mtn School Of Expeditionary Lrng	Expeditionary Boces	Colorado Bocs	80222	317900	4-Other
Paonia High School	Delta County 50(J)	Delta	81428	168900	3-High
Polaris At Ebert Elementary School	Denver County 1	Denver	80205	315000	1-Primary
Teller Elementary School	Denver County 1	Denver	80206	531900	1-Primary
Bromwell Elementary School	Denver County 1	Denver	80209	581000	1-Primary
Lincoln Elementary School	Denver County 1	Denver	80209	581000	1-Primary
Steele Elementary School	Denver County 1	Denver	80209	581000	1-Primary
Cory Elementary School	Denver County 1	Denver	80210	465000	1-Primary
Slavens K-8 School	Denver County 1	Denver	80210	465000	1-Primary

	ELA Prof < 50%	Math Prof < 50%	Grade 3		Grade 4	
Pct Soc Dis			ELA Pct Prof	Math Pct Prof	ELA Pct Prof	Math Pct Prof
32.5	0	0	82.8	89.7	83.2	87.6
19.1	0	0	86.3	86.3	83.0	81.1
31.7	0	0	76.7	78.4	64.1	57.7
5.7	0	0	87.0	93.5	86.9	89.3
18.7	0	0	0.0	0.0	0.0	0.0
15.0	0	1	0.0	0.0	0.0	0.0
26.6	0	0	0.0	0.0	0.0	0.0
26.2	0	0	74.6	70.6	66.3	77.9
30.9	0	2	0.0	0.0	0.0	0.0
24.1	0	0	72.6	78.7	65.4	73.1
23.5	0	2	0.0	0.0	0.0	0.0
18.0	0	0	80.0	76.7	71.2	81.2
3.9	0	0	83.2	79.4	87.9	87.1
23.8	0	0	79.7	71.2	75.4	83.1
14.5	0	1	0.0	0.0	0.0	0.0
14.7	0	0	0.0	0.0	0.0	0.0
7.2	0	0	87.2	85.6	83.9	82.8
15.2	0	0	85.7	89.3	87.5	91.8
16.3	0	1	0.0	0.0	0.0	0.0
16.4	0	0	79.0	69.1	63.7	64.8
16.0	0	0	0.0	0.0	0.0	0.0
30.5	0	2	0.0	0.0	0.0	0.0
24.3	0	2	0.0	0.0	0.0	0.0
29.8	0	0	0.0	0.0	0.0	0.0
12.2	0	0	97.1	76.5	71.4	80.0
0.0	0	2	87.0	91.7	64.0	84.0
25.9	0	2	0.0	0.0	0.0	0.0
6.0	0	0	100.0	100.0	98.7	100.0
33.0	0	0	79.7	78.4	66.7	73.3
7.8	0	0	88.5	92.3	94.5	96.4
28.0	0	0	82.3	72.5	78.0	73.2
15.5	0	0	87.7	91.6	91.8	91.8
10.1	0	0	96.3	93.9	97.4	98.7
7.7	0	0	93.4	92.1	90.0	91.4

	Grade 5		Grade 6	
School Name	ELA Pct Prof	Math Pct Prof	ELA Pct Prof	Math Pct Prof
Eagle Crest Elementary School	85.3	82.3	0.0	0.0
Hygiene Elementary School	64.6	52.1	0.0	0.0
Longmont Estates Elementary School	80.6	67.2	0.0	0.0
Niwot Elementary School	89.1	82.6	0.0	0.0
Niwot High School	0.0	0.0	0.0	0.0
Silver Creek High School	0.0	0.0	0.0	0.0
Westview Middle School	0.0	0.0	82.1	71.1
Alpine Elementary School	67.1	64.7	0.0	0.0
Frederick Senior High School	0.0	0.0	0.0	0.0
Legacy Elementary School	82.3	72.2	0.0	0.0
Mead High School	0.0	0.0	0.0	0.0
Prairie Ridge Elementary School	77.1	68.8	0.0	0.0
Black Rock Elementary	93.5	85.0	0.0	0.0
Erie Elementary School	76.3	67.5	0.0	0.0
Erie High School	0.0	0.0	0.0	0.0
Erie Middle School	0.0	0.0	90.9	80.2
Red Hawk Elementary	84.5	79.8	0.0	0.0
Lyons Elementary School	81.5	75.9	0.0	0.0
Lyons Middle/Senior High School	0.0	0.0	86.5	60.4
Mead Elementary School	79.3	73.0	0.0	0.0
Mead Middle School	0.0	0.0	86.6	79.1
Buena Vista High School	0.0	0.0	0.0	0.0
Clear Creek High School	0.0	0.0	0.0	0.0
Clear Creek Middle School	0.0	0.0	0.0	0.0
King-Murphy Elementary School	81.8	72.7	85.0	55.0
Rocky Mtn School Of Expeditionary Lrng	80.0	76.0	91.5	74.5
Paonia High School	0.0	0.0	0.0	0.0
Polaris At Ebert Elementary School	98.7	98.7	0.0	0.0
Teller Elementary School	82.9	77.1	0.0	0.0
Bromwell Elementary School	92.7	88.1	0.0	0.0
Lincoln Elementary School	88.4	81.4	0.0	0.0
Steele Elementary School	89.2	90.8	0.0	0.0
Cory Elementary School	97.4	94.7	0.0	0.0
Slavens K-8 School	94.2	96.2	93.4	90.8

Grade 7		Grade 8		Grade 9		Grade 10	
ELA Pct Prof	Math Pct Prof	ELA Pct Prof	Math Pct Prof	ELA Pct Prof	Math Pct Prof	ELA Pct Prof	Math Pct Prof
0.0	0.0	0.0	0.0	0.0	0.0	0.0	0.0
0.0	0.0	0.0	0.0	0.0	0.0	0.0	0.0
0.0	0.0	0.0	0.0	0.0	0.0	0.0	0.0
0.0	0.0	0.0	0.0	0.0	0.0	0.0	0.0
0.0	0.0	0.0	0.0	83.3	61.1	83.9	58.6
0.0	0.0	0.0	0.0	80.6	60.5	82.1	48.3
76.8	66.4	81.6	67.0	0.0	0.0	0.0	0.0
0.0	0.0	0.0	0.0	0.0	0.0	0.0	0.0
0.0	0.0	0.0	0.0	59.3	27.9	57.9	22.1
0.0	0.0	0.0	0.0	0.0	0.0	0.0	0.0
0.0	0.0	0.0	0.0	73.3	43.4	73.7	33.0
0.0	0.0	0.0	0.0	0.0	0.0	0.0	0.0
0.0	0.0	0.0	0.0	0.0	0.0	0.0	0.0
0.0	0.0	0.0	0.0	0.0	0.0	0.0	0.0
0.0	0.0	0.0	0.0	78.6	53.3	77.0	39.9
84.2	72.5	77.1	62.6	0.0	0.0	0.0	0.0
0.0	0.0	0.0	0.0	0.0	0.0	0.0	0.0
0.0	0.0	0.0	0.0	0.0	0.0	0.0	0.0
66.7	68.8	84.6	68.0	73.6	41.5	94.7	64.9
0.0	0.0	0.0	0.0	0.0	0.0	0.0	0.0
82.5	80.4	88.6	80.5	0.0	0.0	0.0	0.0
0.0	0.0	0.0	0.0	72.1	32.8	83.3	36.4
0.0	0.0	0.0	0.0	77.4	43.5	75.4	24.6
77.8	58.1	82.5	57.8	0.0	0.0	0.0	0.0
0.0	0.0	0.0	0.0	0.0	0.0	0.0	0.0
94.0	76.5	78.3	63.0	70.8	37.5	85.7	27.3
82.1	71.4	72.5	60.0	76.3	50.0	80.5	40.5
0.0	0.0	0.0	0.0	0.0	0.0	0.0	0.0
0.0	0.0	0.0	0.0	0.0	0.0	0.0	0.0
0.0	0.0	0.0	0.0	0.0	0.0	0.0	0.0
0.0	0.0	0.0	0.0	0.0	0.0	0.0	0.0
0.0	0.0	0.0	0.0	0.0	0.0	0.0	0.0
0.0	0.0	0.0	0.0	0.0	0.0	0.0	0.0
96.2	94.3	92.0	96.0	0.0	0.0	0.0	0.0

School Name	District Name	County Name	Zip Code	Median Home Value (k)	School Level
Denver Online High School	Denver County 1	Denver	80211	389500	3-High
Carson Elementary School	Denver County 1	Denver	80220	402000	1-Primary
Denver School Of The Arts	Denver County 1	Denver	80220	402000	4-Other
Park Hill School	Denver County 1	Denver	80220	402000	1-Primary
Steck Elementary School	Denver County 1	Denver	80220	402000	1-Primary
Southmoor Elementary School	Denver County 1	Denver	80237	352200	1-Primary
Swigert International School	Denver County 1	Denver	80238	495200	
Westerly Creek Elementary	Denver County 1	Denver	80238	495200	1-Primary
William (BILL) Roberts K-8 School	Denver County 1	Denver	80238	495200	1-Primary
Dove Creek High School	Dolores County Re No.2	Dolores	81324	120800	3-High
Castle Rock Elementary School	Douglas County Re 1	Douglas	80104	294000	1-Primary
Douglas County High School	Douglas County Re 1	Douglas	80104	294000	3-High
Edcsd: Colorado Cyber School	Douglas County Re 1	Douglas	80104	294000	4-Other
Flagstone Elementary School	Douglas County Re 1	Douglas	80104	294000	1-Primary
Mesa Middle School	Douglas County Re 1	Douglas	80104	294000	2-Middle
Renaissance Expedition Learn Outward Bound School	Douglas County Re 1	Douglas	80104	294000	1-Primary
Rock Ridge Elementary School	Douglas County Re 1	Douglas	80104	294000	1-Primary
Buffalo Ridge Elementary School	Douglas County Re 1	Douglas	80108	521800	1-Primary
Sage Canyon Elementary	Douglas County Re 1	Douglas	80108	521800	1-Primary
Timber Trail Elementary School	Douglas County Re 1	Douglas	80108	521800	1-Primary
Castle Rock Middle School	Douglas County Re 1	Douglas	80109	373500	2-Middle
Castle View High School	Douglas County Re 1	Douglas	80109	373500	3-High
Clear Sky Elementary	Douglas County Re 1	Douglas	80109	373500	1-Primary
Meadow View Elementary School	Douglas County Re 1	Douglas	80109	373500	1-Primary
Soaring Hawk Elementary School	Douglas County Re 1	Douglas	80109	373500	1-Primary
Franktown Elementary School	Douglas County Re 1	Douglas	80116	527500	1-Primary
Larkspur Elementary School	Douglas County Re 1	Douglas	80118	510600	1-Primary
Acres Green Elementary School	Douglas County Re 1	Douglas	80124	450900	1-Primary
Eagle Ridge Elementary School	Douglas County Re 1	Douglas	80124	450900	1-Primary
Lone Tree Elementary	Douglas County Re 1	Douglas	80124	450900	1-Primary
Rock Canyon High School	Douglas County Re 1	Douglas	80124	450900	3-High
Rocky Heights Middle School	Douglas County Re 1	Douglas	80124	450900	2-Middle
Wildcat Mountain Elementary School	Douglas County Re 1	Douglas	80124	450900	1-Primary
Roxborough Intermediate	Douglas County Re 1	Douglas	80125	386400	1-Primary
Bear Canyon Elementary School	Douglas County Re 1	Douglas	80126	410400	1-Primary

			Grade 3		Grade 4	
Pct Soc Dis	ELA Prof < 50%	Math Prof < 50%	ELA Pct Prof	Math Pct Prof	ELA Pct Prof	Math Pct Prof
29.1	0	2	0.0	0.0	0.0	0.0
15.1	0	0	84.3	80.0	90.9	90.9
14.7	0	0	0.0	0.0	0.0	0.0
28.2	0	0	86.6	82.9	81.1	74.2
8.9	0	0	93.2	93.1	92.7	96.4
29.2	0	0	80.2	78.2	75.0	76.5
6.8	0	0	89.6	85.7	89.8	94.9
16.1	0	0	86.0	90.0	84.8	90.2
16.4	0	0	86.8	86.8	88.8	93.1
32.3	1	2	0.0	0.0	0.0	0.0
23.3	0	0	64.9	55.9	73.6	73.6
13.2	0	2	0.0	0.0	0.0	0.0
9.1	0	2	0.0	0.0	0.0	0.0
13.1	0	0	72.1	74.4	70.2	81.2
20.1	0	0	0.0	0.0	0.0	0.0
4.8	0	0	90.9	87.9	80.0	86.2
18.6	0	0	66.7	73.3	68.0	71.1
4.2	0	0	91.3	93.4	88.7	92.8
6.4	0	0	67.0	68.2	75.2	81.0
3.4	0	0	86.5	91.0	89.1	85.6
14.3	0	0	0.0	0.0	0.0	0.0
12.3	0	2	0.0	0.0	0.0	0.0
16.5	0	0	84.8	84.8	75.9	82.8
7.4	0	0	73.5	66.0	68.1	80.0
7.8	0	0	78.0	72.3	75.0	86.2
9.4	0	0	94.4	90.7	80.8	89.4
12.0	0	0	72.7	65.1	81.6	92.1
18.2	0	0	80.4	88.5	73.6	81.6
11.1	0	0	82.7	87.5	83.8	88.8
5.8	0	0	76.5	83.8	91.7	97.2
2.7	0	0	0.0	0.0	0.0	0.0
3.2	0	0	0.0	0.0	0.0	0.0
3.3	0	0	92.6	93.5	93.5	96.3
11.4	0	0	70.9	75.2	71.7	85.0
6.4	0	0	82.5	90.0	89.0	86.3

School Name	Grade 5		Grade 6	
	ELA Pct Prof	Math Pct Prof	ELA Pct Prof	Math Pct Prof
Denver Online High School	0.0	0.0	0.0	0.0
Carson Elementary School	90.4	91.8	0.0	0.0
Denver School Of The Arts	0.0	0.0	97.0	96.3
Park Hill School	81.8	76.1	0.0	0.0
Steck Elementary School	98.2	98.2	0.0	0.0
Southmoor Elementary School	90.9	84.8	0.0	0.0
Swigert International School	0.0	0.0	0.0	0.0
Westerly Creek Elementary	86.8	80.7	0.0	0.0
William (BILL) Roberts K-8 School	88.7	87.6	78.2	76.4
Dove Creek High School	0.0	0.0	0.0	0.0
Castle Rock Elementary School	81.4	74.6	73.8	61.5
Douglas County High School	0.0	0.0	0.0	0.0
Edcsd: Colorado Cyber School	0.0	0.0	0.0	0.0
Flagstone Elementary School	87.6	85.6	86.7	80.6
Mesa Middle School	0.0	0.0	0.0	0.0
Renaissance Expedition Learn Outward Bound School	93.7	90.5	96.4	80.0
Rock Ridge Elementary School	75.3	65.5	82.8	64.7
Buffalo Ridge Elementary School	91.2	89.2	0.0	0.0
Sage Canyon Elementary	82.8	66.7	87.1	71.8
Timber Trail Elementary School	85.9	90.2	0.0	0.0
Castle Rock Middle School	0.0	0.0	0.0	0.0
Castle View High School	0.0	0.0	0.0	0.0
Clear Sky Elementary	78.1	74.0	82.3	69.6
Meadow View Elementary School	66.7	62.3	81.9	68.7
Soaring Hawk Elementary School	81.4	81.4	89.5	80.2
Franktown Elementary School	86.3	76.5	0.0	0.0
Larkspur Elementary School	88.5	75.0	84.2	66.7
Acres Green Elementary School	84.5	84.5	87.4	67.4
Eagle Ridge Elementary School	88.5	78.4	92.9	81.2
Lone Tree Elementary	90.3	86.1	80.7	82.3
Rock Canyon High School	0.0	0.0	0.0	0.0
Rocky Heights Middle School	0.0	0.0	89.5	87.8
Wildcat Mountain Elementary School	92.6	88.9	0.0	0.0
Roxborough Intermediate	76.6	64.0	83.5	74.3
Bear Canyon Elementary School	94.4	80.9	87.2	65.1

Grade 7		Grade 8		Grade 9		Grade 10	
ELA Pct Prof	Math Pct Prof	ELA Pct Prof	Math Pct Prof	ELA Pct Prof	Math Pct Prof	ELA Pct Prof	Math Pct Prof
0.0	0.0	0.0	0.0	76.2	42.9	70.8	8.3
0.0	0.0	0.0	0.0	0.0	0.0	0.0	0.0
97.1	91.2	96.8	90.5	93.6	73.4	93.4	57.2
0.0	0.0	0.0	0.0	0.0	0.0	0.0	0.0
0.0	0.0	0.0	0.0	0.0	0.0	0.0	0.0
0.0	0.0	0.0	0.0	0.0	0.0	0.0	0.0
0.0	0.0	0.0	0.0	0.0	0.0	0.0	0.0
0.0	0.0	0.0	0.0	0.0	0.0	0.0	0.0
76.2	64.3	71.1	60.0	0.0	0.0	0.0	0.0
47.6	28.6	0.0	0.0	0.0	0.0	70.0	5.0
0.0	0.0	0.0	0.0	0.0	0.0	0.0	0.0
0.0	0.0	0.0	0.0	80.1	49.1	81.8	45.5
0.0	0.0	77.8	61.1	76.5	35.3	90.5	28.6
0.0	0.0	0.0	0.0	0.0	0.0	0.0	0.0
74.1	59.6	74.1	60.9	0.0	0.0	0.0	0.0
0.0	0.0	0.0	0.0	0.0	0.0	0.0	0.0
0.0	0.0	0.0	0.0	0.0	0.0	0.0	0.0
0.0	0.0	0.0	0.0	0.0	0.0	0.0	0.0
0.0	0.0	0.0	0.0	0.0	0.0	0.0	0.0
0.0	0.0	0.0	0.0	0.0	0.0	0.0	0.0
78.1	63.7	74.5	60.3	0.0	0.0	0.0	0.0
0.0	0.0	0.0	0.0	69.7	49.3	73.2	41.9
0.0	0.0	0.0	0.0	0.0	0.0	0.0	0.0
0.0	0.0	0.0	0.0	0.0	0.0	0.0	0.0
0.0	0.0	0.0	0.0	0.0	0.0	0.0	0.0
0.0	0.0	0.0	0.0	0.0	0.0	0.0	0.0
0.0	0.0	0.0	0.0	0.0	0.0	0.0	0.0
0.0	0.0	0.0	0.0	0.0	0.0	0.0	0.0
0.0	0.0	0.0	0.0	0.0	0.0	0.0	0.0
0.0	0.0	0.0	0.0	0.0	0.0	0.0	0.0
0.0	0.0	0.0	0.0	88.7	63.9	91.6	51.5
83.1	80.3	87.8	81.1	0.0	0.0	0.0	0.0
0.0	0.0	0.0	0.0	0.0	0.0	0.0	0.0
0.0	0.0	0.0	0.0	0.0	0.0	0.0	0.0
0.0	0.0	0.0	0.0	0.0	0.0	0.0	0.0

School Name	District Name	County Name	Zip Code	Median Home Value (k)	School Level
Copper Mesa Elementary School	Douglas County Re 1	Douglas	80126	410400	1-Primary
Cougar Run Elementary School	Douglas County Re 1	Douglas	80126	410400	1-Primary
Heritage Elementary School	Douglas County Re 1	Douglas	80126	410400	1-Primary
Mountain Ridge Middle School	Douglas County Re 1	Douglas	80126	410400	2-Middle
Mountain Vista High School	Douglas County Re 1	Douglas	80126	410400	3-High
Northridge Elementary School	Douglas County Re 1	Douglas	80126	410400	1-Primary
Ponderosa High School	Douglas County Re 1	Douglas	80126	410400	3-High
Sand Creek Elementary School	Douglas County Re 1	Douglas	80126	410400	1-Primary
Summit View Elementary School	Douglas County Re 1	Douglas	80126	410400	1-Primary
Coyote Creek Elementary School	Douglas County Re 1	Douglas	80129	372500	1-Primary
Eldorado Elementary School	Douglas County Re 1	Douglas	80129	372500	1-Primary
Ranch View Middle School	Douglas County Re 1	Douglas	80129	372500	2-Middle
Saddle Ranch Elementary School	Douglas County Re 1	Douglas	80129	372500	1-Primary
Stone Mountain Elementary	Douglas County Re 1	Douglas	80129	372500	1-Primary
Thunderridge High School	Douglas County Re 1	Douglas	80129	372500	3-High
Trailblazer Elementary School	Douglas County Re 1	Douglas	80129	372500	1-Primary
Arrowwood Elementary School	Douglas County Re 1	Douglas	80130	391900	1-Primary
Cresthill Middle School	Douglas County Re 1	Douglas	80130	391900	2-Middle
Fox Creek Elementary School	Douglas County Re 1	Douglas	80130	391900	1-Primary
Highlands Ranch High School	Douglas County Re 1	Douglas	80130	391900	3-High
Redstone Elementary School	Douglas County Re 1	Douglas	80130	391900	1-Primary
Chaparral High School	Douglas County Re 1	Douglas	80134	369600	3-High
Cherokee Trail Elementary School	Douglas County Re 1	Douglas	80134	369600	1-Primary
Gold Rush Elementary	Douglas County Re 1	Douglas	80134	369600	1-Primary
Legacy Point Elementary School	Douglas County Re 1	Douglas	80134	369600	1-Primary
Mammoth Heights Elementary	Douglas County Re 1	Douglas	80134	369600	1-Primary
Northeast Elementary School	Douglas County Re 1	Douglas	80134	369600	1-Primary
Pine Grove Elementary School	Douglas County Re 1	Douglas	80134	369600	1-Primary
Prairie Crossing Elementary School	Douglas County Re 1	Douglas	80134	369600	1-Primary
Sagewood Middle School	Douglas County Re 1	Douglas	80134	369600	2-Middle
Cimarron Middle	Douglas County Re 1	Douglas	80138	397900	2-Middle
Frontier Valley Elementary School	Douglas County Re 1	Douglas	80138	397900	1-Primary
Iron Horse Elementary School	Douglas County Re 1	Douglas	80138	397900	1-Primary
Legend High School	Douglas County Re 1	Douglas	80138	397900	3-High
Pine Lane Elementary	Douglas County Re 1	Douglas	80138	397900	1-Primary
Pioneer Elementary School	Douglas County Re 1	Douglas	80138	397900	1-Primary

Pct Soc Dis	ELA Prof < 50%	Math Prof < 50%	Grade 3		Grade 4	
			ELA Pct Prof	Math Pct Prof	ELA Pct Prof	Math Pct Prof
2.3	0	0	80.0	80.2	84.7	85.9
10.5	0	0	84.6	87.9	85.7	94.0
3.8	0	0	89.5	89.5	90.9	90.9
8.1	0	0	0.0	0.0	0.0	0.0
6.0	0	1	0.0	0.0	0.0	0.0
11.5	0	0	79.6	85.6	97.1	93.3
8.6	0	1	0.0	0.0	0.0	0.0
12.3	0	0	80.8	84.7	80.6	86.0
6.0	0	0	81.7	88.7	86.8	86.8
6.0	0	0	78.1	85.9	83.6	87.3
6.7	0	0	80.4	84.7	80.6	87.5
6.4	0	0	0.0	0.0	0.0	0.0
3.0	0	0	86.4	81.8	88.9	96.3
1.7	0	0	90.1	93.4	89.2	90.4
7.3	0	0	0.0	0.0	0.0	0.0
9.0	0	0	85.1	88.1	84.0	85.2
11.2	0	0	77.1	80.8	78.3	87.0
13.3	0	0	0.0	0.0	0.0	0.0
6.5	0	0	85.5	82.1	70.2	80.0
9.4	0	1	0.0	0.0	0.0	0.0
1.8	0	0	89.9	92.9	79.6	90.4
11.0	0	1	0.0	0.0	0.0	0.0
14.1	0	0	81.2	77.6	75.4	77.9
7.4	0	0	82.3	83.2	72.6	77.9
12.9	0	0	86.2	79.8	82.3	88.4
11.9	0	0	77.6	77.4	78.8	75.6
5.7	0	0	85.0	88.7	82.6	87.7
4.8	0	0	90.8	80.5	88.2	88.2
7.8	0	0	77.5	76.1	78.1	81.0
8.1	0	0	0.0	0.0	0.0	0.0
9.8	0	0	0.0	0.0	0.0	0.0
6.5	0	0	83.6	87.3	65.0	81.3
13.7	0	0	82.0	81.0	81.5	90.7
8.6	0	1	0.0	0.0	0.0	0.0
25.2	0	0	68.5	67.3	75.8	77.2
15.4	0	0	73.7	78.0	65.0	69.3

School Name	Grade 5		Grade 6	
	ELA Pct Prof	Math Pct Prof	ELA Pct Prof	Math Pct Prof
Copper Mesa Elementary School	88.2	87.1	89.0	79.0
Cougar Run Elementary School	88.4	81.4	93.2	83.6
Heritage Elementary School	94.7	95.8	97.7	96.5
Mountain Ridge Middle School	0.0	0.0	0.0	0.0
Mountain Vista High School	0.0	0.0	0.0	0.0
Northridge Elementary School	90.2	92.0	94.3	88.6
Ponderosa High School	0.0	0.0	0.0	0.0
Sand Creek Elementary School	81.4	75.9	81.2	80.0
Summit View Elementary School	90.2	88.0	90.3	94.4
Coyote Creek Elementary School	84.3	84.3	84.9	79.2
Eldorado Elementary School	89.4	87.2	85.1	79.3
Ranch View Middle School	0.0	0.0	0.0	0.0
Saddle Ranch Elementary School	98.8	89.0	89.2	90.3
Stone Mountain Elementary	95.1	91.2	93.6	92.5
Thunderridge High School	0.0	0.0	0.0	0.0
Trailblazer Elementary School	83.0	86.8	91.9	83.9
Arrowwood Elementary School	81.2	70.6	81.4	66.7
Cresthill Middle School	0.0	0.0	0.0	0.0
Fox Creek Elementary School	72.0	70.7	93.2	88.0
Highlands Ranch High School	0.0	0.0	0.0	0.0
Redstone Elementary School	94.4	92.2	0.0	0.0
Chaparral High School	0.0	0.0	0.0	0.0
Cherokee Trail Elementary School	79.2	76.0	83.5	70.5
Gold Rush Elementary	90.5	83.8	0.0	0.0
Legacy Point Elementary School	81.7	84.2	0.0	0.0
Mammoth Heights Elementary	81.2	69.2	82.6	72.1
Northeast Elementary School	83.9	82.3	0.0	0.0
Pine Grove Elementary School	92.3	87.5	90.7	87.2
Prairie Crossing Elementary School	72.2	67.1	88.1	67.7
Sagewood Middle School	0.0	0.0	87.2	71.6
Cimarron Middle	0.0	0.0	85.0	81.7
Frontier Valley Elementary School	86.0	83.5	0.0	0.0
Iron Horse Elementary School	79.1	80.2	0.0	0.0
Legend High School	0.0	0.0	0.0	0.0
Pine Lane Elementary	75.5	73.0	83.7	73.3
Pioneer Elementary School	75.7	67.0	0.0	0.0

Grade 7		Grade 8		Grade 9		Grade 10	
ELA Pct Prof	Math Pct Prof	ELA Pct Prof	Math Pct Prof	ELA Pct Prof	Math Pct Prof	ELA Pct Prof	Math Pct Prof
0.0	0.0	0.0	0.0	0.0	0.0	0.0	0.0
0.0	0.0	0.0	0.0	0.0	0.0	0.0	0.0
0.0	0.0	0.0	0.0	0.0	0.0	0.0	0.0
86.7	82.7	86.0	75.5	0.0	0.0	0.0	0.0
0.0	0.0	0.0	0.0	87.0	66.6	83.9	48.4
0.0	0.0	0.0	0.0	0.0	0.0	0.0	0.0
0.0	0.0	0.0	0.0	74.9	50.7	83.5	46.0
0.0	0.0	0.0	0.0	0.0	0.0	0.0	0.0
0.0	0.0	0.0	0.0	0.0	0.0	0.0	0.0
0.0	0.0	0.0	0.0	0.0	0.0	0.0	0.0
0.0	0.0	0.0	0.0	0.0	0.0	0.0	0.0
84.2	73.1	83.2	69.2	0.0	0.0	0.0	0.0
0.0	0.0	0.0	0.0	0.0	0.0	0.0	0.0
0.0	0.0	0.0	0.0	0.0	0.0	0.0	0.0
0.0	0.0	0.0	0.0	79.6	59.6	85.7	52.1
0.0	0.0	0.0	0.0	0.0	0.0	0.0	0.0
0.0	0.0	0.0	0.0	0.0	0.0	0.0	0.0
82.3	65.7	79.6	60.2	0.0	0.0	0.0	0.0
0.0	0.0	0.0	0.0	0.0	0.0	0.0	0.0
0.0	0.0	0.0	0.0	70.7	53.0	72.5	44.9
0.0	0.0	0.0	0.0	0.0	0.0	0.0	0.0
0.0	0.0	0.0	0.0	75.6	53.0	77.4	46.0
0.0	0.0	0.0	0.0	0.0	0.0	0.0	0.0
0.0	0.0	0.0	0.0	0.0	0.0	0.0	0.0
0.0	0.0	0.0	0.0	0.0	0.0	0.0	0.0
0.0	0.0	0.0	0.0	0.0	0.0	0.0	0.0
0.0	0.0	0.0	0.0	0.0	0.0	0.0	0.0
0.0	0.0	0.0	0.0	0.0	0.0	0.0	0.0
0.0	0.0	0.0	0.0	0.0	0.0	0.0	0.0
85.1	72.6	80.9	66.1	0.0	0.0	0.0	0.0
83.1	75.2	80.2	68.9	0.0	0.0	0.0	0.0
0.0	0.0	0.0	0.0	0.0	0.0	0.0	0.0
0.0	0.0	0.0	0.0	0.0	0.0	0.0	0.0
0.0	0.0	0.0	0.0	87.5	60.2	85.6	48.5
0.0	0.0	0.0	0.0	0.0	0.0	0.0	0.0
0.0	0.0	0.0	0.0	0.0	0.0	0.0	0.0

School Name	District Name	County Name	Zip Code	Median Home Value (k)	School Level
Sierra Middle School	Douglas County Re 1	Douglas	80138	397900	2-Middle
Brush Creek Elementary School	Eagle County Re 50	Eagle	81631	425200	1-Primary
Eagle Valley Middle School	Eagle County Re 50	Eagle	81631	425200	2-Middle
Red Sandstone Elementary School	Eagle County Re 50	Eagle	81657	839100	1-Primary
Air Academy High School	Academy 20	El Paso	80840	260559	3-High
Edith Wolford Elementary School	Academy 20	El Paso	80908	397800	1-Primary
Pine Creek High School	Academy 20	El Paso	80908	397800	3-High
Eagleview Middle School	Academy 20	El Paso	80919	311600	2-Middle
Foothills Elementary School	Academy 20	El Paso	80919	311600	1-Primary
Rockrimmon Elementary School	Academy 20	El Paso	80919	311600	1-Primary
Woodmen-Roberts Elementary School	Academy 20	El Paso	80919	311600	1-Primary
Academy Endeavour Elementary School	Academy 20	El Paso	80920	271800	1-Primary
Academy International Elementary School	Academy 20	El Paso	80920	271800	1-Primary
Challenger Middle School	Academy 20	El Paso	80920	271800	2-Middle
Explorer Elementary School	Academy 20	El Paso	80920	271800	1-Primary
Liberty High School	Academy 20	El Paso	80920	271800	3-High
Mountain Ridge Middle School	Academy 20	El Paso	80920	271800	2-Middle
Mountain View Elementary School	Academy 20	El Paso	80920	271800	1-Primary
Prairie Hills Elementary School	Academy 20	El Paso	80920	271800	1-Primary
Rampart High School	Academy 20	El Paso	80920	271800	3-High
Timberview Middle School	Academy 20	El Paso	80920	271800	2-Middle
Antelope Trails Elementary School	Academy 20	El Paso	80921	366200	1-Primary
Discovery Canyon Campus School	Academy 20	El Paso	80921	366200	4-Other
The Da Vinci Academy School	Academy 20	El Paso	80921	366200	1-Primary
Chinook Trail Elementary School	Academy 20	El Paso	80924	376700	1-Primary
Ranch Creek Elementary	Academy 20	El Paso	80924	376700	1-Primary
Gold Camp Elementary School	Cheyenne Mountain 12	El Paso	80905	166300	1-Primary
Broadmoor Elementary School	Cheyenne Mountain 12	El Paso	80906	287800	1-Primary
Cheyenne Mountain Elementary School	Cheyenne Mountain 12	El Paso	80906	287800	1-Primary
Cheyenne Mountain High School	Cheyenne Mountain 12	El Paso	80906	287800	3-High
Cheyenne Mountain Junior High School	Cheyenne Mountain 12	El Paso	80906	287800	2-Middle

			Grade 3		Grade 4	
Pct Soc Dis	ELA Prof < 50%	Math Prof < 50%	ELA Pct Prof	Math Pct Prof	ELA Pct Prof	Math Pct Prof
15.4	0	0	0.0	0.0	0.0	0.0
17.6	0	0	90.3	82.3	75.0	73.8
29.1	0	0	0.0	0.0	0.0	0.0
29.6	0	0	80.0	70.0	78.0	61.9
10.3	0	1	0.0	0.0	0.0	0.0
12.1	0	0	78.3	71.7	85.0	86.6
5.2	0	1	0.0	0.0	0.0	0.0
15.8	0	0	0.0	0.0	0.0	0.0
18.9	0	0	85.4	85.2	80.6	75.0
19.9	0	0	86.8	79.7	89.5	92.9
8.3	0	0	82.2	82.2	86.0	79.1
14.3	0	0	78.6	75.2	86.1	89.1
7.5	0	0	91.7	86.5	89.5	88.4
8.5	0	0	0.0	0.0	0.0	0.0
13.8	0	0	93.6	94.9	87.2	87.2
10.7	0	1	0.0	0.0	0.0	0.0
20.1	0	0	0.0	0.0	0.0	0.0
6.4	0	0	86.8	88.0	92.0	90.2
21.9	0	0	81.0	68.3	71.8	67.6
12.3	0	2	0.0	0.0	0.0	0.0
16.9	0	0	0.0	0.0	0.0	0.0
10.8	0	0	79.8	76.2	83.2	83.0
7.5	0	1	87.7	93.8	79.1	84.9
12.8	0	0	88.7	91.5	86.2	80.4
6.4	0	0	88.6	91.3	89.0	86.6
12.7	0	0	79.2	81.6	84.8	79.8
12.6	0	0	88.5	95.2	92.6	93.8
11.8	0	0	98.0	94.0	90.0	94.0
5.4	0	0	98.0	100.0	95.7	100.0
9.3	0	0	0.0	0.0	0.0	0.0
14.4	0	0	0.0	0.0	0.0	0.0

School Name	Grade 5		Grade 6	
	ELA Pct Prof	Math Pct Prof	ELA Pct Prof	Math Pct Prof
Sierra Middle School	0.0	0.0	0.0	0.0
Brush Creek Elementary School	94.6	83.0	0.0	0.0
Eagle Valley Middle School	0.0	0.0	86.2	80.6
Red Sandstone Elementary School	85.0	80.0	0.0	0.0
Air Academy High School	0.0	0.0	0.0	0.0
Edith Wolford Elementary School	75.5	54.7	0.0	0.0
Pine Creek High School	0.0	0.0	0.0	0.0
Eagleview Middle School	0.0	0.0	82.5	75.2
Foothills Elementary School	85.1	80.8	0.0	0.0
Rockrimmon Elementary School	88.9	80.2	0.0	0.0
Woodmen-Roberts Elementary School	91.0	91.0	0.0	0.0
Academy Endeavour Elementary School	88.7	82.9	0.0	0.0
Academy International Elementary School	90.8	85.7	0.0	0.0
Challenger Middle School	0.0	0.0	89.2	82.4
Explorer Elementary School	90.2	87.8	0.0	0.0
Liberty High School	0.0	0.0	0.0	0.0
Mountain Ridge Middle School	0.0	0.0	80.7	69.8
Mountain View Elementary School	91.5	88.0	0.0	0.0
Prairie Hills Elementary School	80.0	66.7	0.0	0.0
Rampart High School	0.0	0.0	0.0	0.0
Timberview Middle School	0.0	0.0	83.2	77.4
Antelope Trails Elementary School	92.9	82.1	0.0	0.0
Discovery Canyon Campus School	86.4	84.5	86.2	83.7
The Da Vinci Academy School	89.8	78.4	0.0	0.0
Chinook Trail Elementary School	92.3	83.5	0.0	0.0
Ranch Creek Elementary	82.3	77.7	0.0	0.0
Gold Camp Elementary School	95.9	94.5	94.6	86.5
Broadmoor Elementary School	91.3	91.3	93.6	85.1
Cheyenne Mountain Elementary School	92.0	94.0	98.2	94.4
Cheyenne Mountain High School	0.0	0.0	0.0	0.0
Cheyenne Mountain Junior High School	0.0	0.0	0.0	0.0

Grade 7		Grade 8		Grade 9		Grade 10	
ELA Pct Prof	Math Pct Prof	ELA Pct Prof	Math Pct Prof	ELA Pct Prof	Math Pct Prof	ELA Pct Prof	Math Pct Prof
79.4	64.9	75.2	65.3	0.0	0.0	0.0	0.0
0.0	0.0	0.0	0.0	0.0	0.0	0.0	0.0
79.6	77.8	84.2	59.8	0.0	0.0	0.0	0.0
0.0	0.0	0.0	0.0	0.0	0.0	0.0	0.0
0.0	0.0	0.0	0.0	89.7	58.0	92.0	49.1
0.0	0.0	0.0	0.0	0.0	0.0	0.0	0.0
0.0	0.0	0.0	0.0	86.7	57.6	88.5	49.4
78.7	67.8	82.8	64.4	0.0	0.0	0.0	0.0
0.0	0.0	0.0	0.0	0.0	0.0	0.0	0.0
0.0	0.0	0.0	0.0	0.0	0.0	0.0	0.0
0.0	0.0	0.0	0.0	0.0	0.0	0.0	0.0
0.0	0.0	0.0	0.0	0.0	0.0	0.0	0.0
0.0	0.0	0.0	0.0	0.0	0.0	0.0	0.0
90.3	74.8	90.4	74.6	0.0	0.0	0.0	0.0
0.0	0.0	0.0	0.0	0.0	0.0	0.0	0.0
0.0	0.0	0.0	0.0	85.4	51.9	89.1	46.6
81.9	69.5	74.6	64.8	0.0	0.0	0.0	0.0
0.0	0.0	0.0	0.0	0.0	0.0	0.0	0.0
0.0	0.0	0.0	0.0	0.0	0.0	0.0	0.0
0.0	0.0	0.0	0.0	80.6	49.7	81.9	46.8
77.1	67.3	84.6	70.4	0.0	0.0	0.0	0.0
0.0	0.0	0.0	0.0	0.0	0.0	0.0	0.0
87.1	80.4	81.3	67.1	90.4	57.4	89.5	48.6
0.0	0.0	0.0	0.0	0.0	0.0	0.0	0.0
0.0	0.0	0.0	0.0	0.0	0.0	0.0	0.0
0.0	0.0	0.0	0.0	0.0	0.0	0.0	0.0
0.0	0.0	0.0	0.0	0.0	0.0	0.0	0.0
0.0	0.0	0.0	0.0	0.0	0.0	0.0	0.0
0.0	0.0	0.0	0.0	0.0	0.0	0.0	0.0
0.0	0.0	0.0	0.0	87.5	74.5	86.9	67.4
87.5	81.1	88.3	78.8	0.0	0.0	0.0	0.0

School Name	District Name	County Name	Zip Code	Median Home Value (k)	School Level
Pinon Valley Elementary School	Cheyenne Mountain 12	El Paso	80906	287800	1-Primary
Buena Vista Elementary School	Colorado Springs 11	El Paso	80905	166300	1-Primary
Steele Elementary School	Colorado Springs 11	El Paso	80907	194100	1-Primary
Achievek12	Colorado Springs 11	El Paso	80909	169500	4-Other
Jenkins Middle School	Colorado Springs 11	El Paso	80918	214000	2-Middle
Martinez Elementary School	Colorado Springs 11	El Paso	80918	214000	1-Primary
Scott Elementary School	Colorado Springs 11	El Paso	80918	214000	1-Primary
Chipeta Elementary School	Colorado Springs 11	El Paso	80919	311600	1-Primary
Falcon High School	Falcon 49	El Paso	80831	267300	3-High
Falcon Middle School	Falcon 49	El Paso	80831	267300	2-Middle
Meridian Ranch International School	Falcon 49	El Paso	80831	267300	1-Primary
Woodmen Hills Elementary School	Falcon 49	El Paso	80831	267300	1-Primary
Falcon Virtual Academy	Falcon 49	El Paso	80915	173600	4-Other
Remington Elementary School	Falcon 49	El Paso	80922	222300	1-Primary
Sand Creek High School	Falcon 49	El Paso	80922	222300	3-High
Springs Ranch Elementary School	Falcon 49	El Paso	80922	222300	1-Primary
Stetson Elementary School	Falcon 49	El Paso	80922	222300	1-Primary
Ridgeview Elementary School	Falcon 49	El Paso	80923	232700	1-Primary
Skyview Middle School	Falcon 49	El Paso	80923	232700	2-Middle
Vista Ridge High School	Falcon 49	El Paso	80923	232700	3-High
Eagleside Elementary School	Fountain 8	El Paso	80817	182000	1-Primary
Bear Creek Elementary School	Lewis-Palmer 38	El Paso	80132	389300	1-Primary
Lewis-Palmer Elementary School	Lewis-Palmer 38	El Paso	80132	389300	1-Primary
Lewis-Palmer High School	Lewis-Palmer 38	El Paso	80132	389300	3-High
Lewis-Palmer Middle School	Lewis-Palmer 38	El Paso	80132	389300	2-Middle
Palmer Ridge High School	Lewis-Palmer 38	El Paso	80132	389300	3-High
Prairie Winds Elementary School	Lewis-Palmer 38	El Paso	80132	389300	1-Primary
Palmer Lake Elementary School	Lewis-Palmer 38	El Paso	80133	232800	1-Primary
Ray E Kilmer Elementary School	Lewis-Palmer 38	El Paso	80908	397800	1-Primary
Manitou Springs Elementary School	Manitou Springs 14	El Paso	80829	308900	1-Primary
Manitou Springs High School	Manitou Springs 14	El Paso	80829	308900	3-High
Manitou Springs Middle School	Manitou Springs 14	El Paso	80829	308900	2-Middle
Ute Pass Elementary School	Manitou Springs 14	El Paso	80829	308900	1-Primary
Peyton Elementary School	Peyton 23 Jt	El Paso	80831	267300	1-Primary

			Grade 3		Grade 4	
Pct Soc Dis	ELA Prof < 50%	Math Prof < 50%	ELA Pct Prof	Math Pct Prof	ELA Pct Prof	Math Pct Prof
12.6	0	0	84.8	84.8	80.4	83.9
21.4	0	0	85.7	67.9	92.3	84.6
18.9	0	0	92.7	100.0	93.5	97.8
29.6	0	4	0.0	0.0	0.0	0.0
27.3	0	0	0.0	0.0	0.0	0.0
26.2	0	0	75.0	85.1	80.5	85.2
29.1	0	0	80.4	85.0	85.1	89.4
21.0	0	0	92.5	93.8	86.2	94.9
13.3	0	2	0.0	0.0	0.0	0.0
18.4	0	0	0.0	0.0	0.0	0.0
10.8	0	0	76.2	79.5	82.6	79.1
15.6	0	0	72.1	82.5	84.2	84.2
0.2	0	4	52.4	52.4	69.6	78.3
30.4	0	0	73.8	73.8	79.3	84.9
25.7	0	2	0.0	0.0	0.0	0.0
22.2	0	0	74.8	83.8	66.7	69.4
23.7	0	0	73.2	77.3	72.0	72.7
23.0	0	0	76.9	82.6	68.7	66.1
27.0	0	0	0.0	0.0	0.0	0.0
17.7	0	2	0.0	0.0	0.0	0.0
30.1	0	0	79.8	79.6	76.7	86.7
10.3	0	0	84.9	92.4	75.9	83.9
9.0	0	0	90.0	95.1	85.7	82.8
7.8	0	0	0.0	0.0	0.0	0.0
9.6	0	0	0.0	0.0	0.0	0.0
8.6	0	0	0.0	0.0	0.0	0.0
6.0	0	0	91.7	85.4	84.1	84.1
32.7	0	0	75.5	88.0	76.5	85.3
9.9	0	0	75.7	81.1	82.6	89.9
27.5	0	0	84.1	77.5	76.4	72.2
18.9	0	2	0.0	0.0	0.0	0.0
27.8	0	0	0.0	0.0	0.0	0.0
32.7	0	0	0.0	0.0	80.0	76.0
31.4	0	0	81.8	87.9	65.1	69.8

School Name	Grade 5		Grade 6	
	ELA Pct Prof	Math Pct Prof	ELA Pct Prof	Math Pct Prof
Pinon Valley Elementary School	93.9	83.7	94.2	82.7
Buena Vista Elementary School	76.5	70.6	0.0	0.0
Steele Elementary School	91.7	93.8	0.0	0.0
Achievek12	0.0	0.0	0.0	0.0
Jenkins Middle School	0.0	0.0	85.4	70.8
Martinez Elementary School	84.6	75.7	0.0	0.0
Scott Elementary School	79.1	77.4	0.0	0.0
Chipeta Elementary School	93.2	91.9	0.0	0.0
Falcon High School	0.0	0.0	0.0	0.0
Falcon Middle School	0.0	0.0	74.5	59.4
Meridian Ranch International School	86.7	73.5	0.0	0.0
Woodmen Hills Elementary School	80.2	72.2	0.0	0.0
Falcon Virtual Academy	93.3	73.3	81.5	51.9
Remington Elementary School	71.2	62.7	0.0	0.0
Sand Creek High School	0.0	0.0	0.0	0.0
Springs Ranch Elementary School	86.2	74.5	0.0	0.0
Stetson Elementary School	68.4	67.3	0.0	0.0
Ridgeview Elementary School	73.5	60.8	0.0	0.0
Skyview Middle School	0.0	0.0	72.8	54.6
Vista Ridge High School	0.0	0.0	0.0	0.0
Eagleside Elementary School	73.6	68.2	0.0	0.0
Bear Creek Elementary School	86.5	88.2	83.2	76.1
Lewis-Palmer Elementary School	89.4	82.1	85.7	63.6
Lewis-Palmer High School	0.0	0.0	0.0	0.0
Lewis-Palmer Middle School	0.0	0.0	0.0	0.0
Palmer Ridge High School	0.0	0.0	0.0	0.0
Prairie Winds Elementary School	90.8	92.3	90.0	83.3
Palmer Lake Elementary School	87.9	84.8	90.6	73.6
Ray E Kilmer Elementary School	90.0	82.0	92.2	84.3
Manitou Springs Elementary School	82.9	70.7	0.0	0.0
Manitou Springs High School	0.0	0.0	0.0	0.0
Manitou Springs Middle School	0.0	0.0	77.2	67.8
Ute Pass Elementary School	100.0	70.6	0.0	0.0
Peyton Elementary School	76.7	72.1	75.5	51.0

Grade 7		Grade 8		Grade 9		Grade 10	
ELA Pct Prof	Math Pct Prof	ELA Pct Prof	Math Pct Prof	ELA Pct Prof	Math Pct Prof	ELA Pct Prof	Math Pct Prof
0.0	0.0	0.0	0.0	0.0	0.0	0.0	0.0
0.0	0.0	0.0	0.0	0.0	0.0	0.0	0.0
0.0	0.0	0.0	0.0	0.0	0.0	0.0	0.0
66.7	33.3	66.7	33.3	65.0	10.0	67.7	11.8
80.5	68.2	75.9	65.4	0.0	0.0	0.0	0.0
0.0	0.0	0.0	0.0	0.0	0.0	0.0	0.0
0.0	0.0	0.0	0.0	0.0	0.0	0.0	0.0
0.0	0.0	0.0	0.0	0.0	0.0	0.0	0.0
0.0	0.0	0.0	0.0	71.5	39.4	79.9	33.8
73.6	53.5	73.6	58.8	0.0	0.0	0.0	0.0
0.0	0.0	0.0	0.0	0.0	0.0	0.0	0.0
0.0	0.0	0.0	0.0	0.0	0.0	0.0	0.0
74.4	41.0	76.5	30.9	86.8	39.5	69.4	16.3
0.0	0.0	0.0	0.0	0.0	0.0	0.0	0.0
0.0	0.0	0.0	0.0	66.9	26.1	63.9	21.3
0.0	0.0	0.0	0.0	0.0	0.0	0.0	0.0
0.0	0.0	0.0	0.0	0.0	0.0	0.0	0.0
0.0	0.0	0.0	0.0	0.0	0.0	0.0	0.0
71.1	53.9	69.2	57.9	0.0	0.0	0.0	0.0
0.0	0.0	0.0	0.0	70.8	42.5	72.2	30.0
0.0	0.0	0.0	0.0	0.0	0.0	0.0	0.0
0.0	0.0	0.0	0.0	0.0	0.0	0.0	0.0
ELA	Math	ELA	Math	ELA	Math	ELA	Math
0.0	0.0	0.0	0.0	87.7	67.5	87.7	54.2
80.9	71.4	83.4	73.3	0.0	0.0	0.0	0.0
0.0	0.0	0.0	0.0	87.2	66.1	88.7	59.9
0.0	0.0	0.0	0.0	0.0	0.0	0.0	0.0
0.0	0.0	0.0	0.0	0.0	0.0	0.0	0.0
0.0	0.0	0.0	0.0	0.0	0.0	0.0	0.0
0.0	0.0	0.0	0.0	0.0	0.0	0.0	0.0
0.0	0.0	0.0	0.0	74.8	41.0	79.8	28.8
81.8	63.5	69.5	53.5	0.0	0.0	0.0	0.0
0.0	0.0	0.0	0.0	0.0	0.0	0.0	0.0
0.0	0.0	0.0	0.0	0.0	0.0	0.0	0.0

School Name	District Name	County Name	Zip Code	Median Home Value (k)	School Level
Peyton Junior High School	Peyton 23 Jt	El Paso	80831	267300	N-Not Applicable
Peyton Senior High School	Peyton 23 Jt	El Paso	80831	267300	3-High
Elbert Elementary School	Elbert 200	Elbert	80106	346500	1-Primary
Elbert Junior-Senior High School	Elbert 200	Elbert	80106	346500	3-High
Elizabeth High School	Elizabeth C-1	Elbert	80107	346300	3-High
Elizabeth Middle School	Elizabeth C-1	Elbert	80107	346300	2-Middle
Singing Hills Elementary School	Elizabeth C-1	Elbert	80138	397900	1-Primary
Kiowa High School	Kiowa C-2	Elbert	80117	274600	3-High
Kiowa Middle School	Kiowa C-2	Elbert	80117	274600	2-Middle
Glenwood Springs High School	Roaring Fork Re-1	Garfield	81601	372100	3-High
Gilpin County Elementary School	Gilpin County Re-1	Gilpin	80422	318000	1-Primary
Gilpin County Undivided High School	Gilpin County Re-1	Gilpin	80422	318000	4-Other
Fraser Valley Elementary School	East Grand 2	Grand	80442	296600	1-Primary
East Grand Middle School	East Grand 2	Grand	80446	219900	2-Middle
Middle Park High School	East Grand 2	Grand	80446	219900	3-High
Crested Butte Community School	Gunnison Watershed Re1j	Gunnison	81224	680300	4-Other
Gunnison High School	Gunnison Watershed Re1j	Gunnison	81230	291700	3-High
Gunnison Middle School	Gunnison Watershed Re1j	Gunnison	81230	291700	2-Middle
Drake Junior High School	Jefferson County R-1	Jefferson	80002	254400	2-Middle
Hackberry Hill Elementary School	Jefferson County R-1	Jefferson	80003	251500	1-Primary
Arvada West High School	Jefferson County R-1	Jefferson	80004	291300	3-High
Stott Elementary School	Jefferson County R-1	Jefferson	80004	291300	1-Primary
Vanderhoof Elementary School	Jefferson County R-1	Jefferson	80004	291300	1-Primary
Meiklejohn Elementary	Jefferson County R-1	Jefferson	80005	330400	1-Primary
Oberon Junior High School	Jefferson County R-1	Jefferson	80005	330400	2-Middle
Ralston Valley Senior High School	Jefferson County R-1	Jefferson	80005	330400	3-High
Sierra Elementary School	Jefferson County R-1	Jefferson	80005	330400	1-Primary

Pct Soc Dis	ELA Prof < 50%	Math Prof < 50%	Grade 3		Grade 4	
			ELA Pct Prof	Math Pct Prof	ELA Pct Prof	Math Pct Prof
28.4	0	0	0.0	0.0	0.0	0.0
22.4	0	2	0.0	0.0	0.0	0.0
27.5	0	0	0.0	0.0	0.0	0.0
27.0	0	0	0.0	0.0	0.0	0.0
14.5	0	2	0.0	0.0	0.0	0.0
21.4	0	0	0.0	0.0	0.0	0.0
20.3	0	0	67.6	77.1	71.0	72.4
32.8	0	2	0.0	0.0	0.0	0.0
32.9	0	1	0.0	0.0	0.0	0.0
25.4	0	2	0.0	0.0	0.0	0.0
31.6	0	0	81.8	83.9	62.1	62.1
29.1	0	4	0.0	0.0	0.0	0.0
28.8	0	0	95.2	85.7	85.7	91.4
26.9	0	0	0.0	0.0	0.0	0.0
22.8	0	1	0.0	0.0	0.0	0.0
11.8	0	0	82.3	83.1	84.9	94.3
22.0	0	2	0.0	0.0	0.0	0.0
30.2	0	1	0.0	0.0	0.0	0.0
24.0	0	0	0.0	0.0	0.0	0.0
30.4	0	0	71.6	79.0	89.0	87.7
29.4	0	2	0.0	0.0	0.0	0.0
25.3	0	1	79.5	79.5	77.2	75.4
29.3	0	0	77.5	79.2	65.3	69.4
4.2	0	0	95.4	97.7	90.2	90.2
23.1	0	0	0.0	0.0	0.0	0.0
10.7	0	0	0.0	0.0	0.0	0.0
15.4	0	0	95.4	95.4	84.9	83.7

	Grade 5		Grade 6	
School Name	ELA Pct Prof	Math Pct Prof	ELA Pct Prof	Math Pct Prof
Peyton Junior High School	0.0	0.0	0.0	0.0
Peyton Senior High School	0.0	0.0	0.0	0.0
Elbert Elementary School	81.8	68.2	0.0	0.0
Elbert Junior-Senior High School	0.0	0.0	0.0	0.0
Elizabeth High School	0.0	0.0	0.0	0.0
Elizabeth Middle School	0.0	0.0	84.7	68.2
Singing Hills Elementary School	66.2	60.9	0.0	0.0
Kiowa High School	0.0	0.0	0.0	0.0
Kiowa Middle School	0.0	0.0	72.7	72.7
Glenwood Springs High School	0.0	0.0	0.0	0.0
Gilpin County Elementary School	61.3	61.3	0.0	0.0
Gilpin County Undivided High School	0.0	0.0	78.4	48.6
Fraser Valley Elementary School	86.5	83.8	0.0	0.0
East Grand Middle School	0.0	0.0	82.4	70.3
Middle Park High School	0.0	0.0	0.0	0.0
Crested Butte Community School	77.0	74.6	82.3	80.4
Gunnison High School	0.0	0.0	0.0	0.0
Gunnison Middle School	0.0	0.0	75.5	64.7
Drake Junior High School	0.0	0.0	0.0	0.0
Hackberry Hill Elementary School	83.3	75.0	81.2	75.3
Arvada West High School	0.0	0.0	0.0	0.0
Stott Elementary School	85.0	82.5	64.5	45.2
Vanderhoof Elementary School	84.3	78.6	84.8	80.4
Meiklejohn Elementary	95.7	94.6	91.8	87.1
Oberon Junior High School	0.0	0.0	0.0	0.0
Ralston Valley Senior High School	0.0	0.0	0.0	0.0
Sierra Elementary School	94.1	87.1	92.0	81.6

Grade 7		Grade 8		Grade 9		Grade 10	
ELA Pct Prof	Math Pct Prof	ELA Pct Prof	Math Pct Prof	ELA Pct Prof	Math Pct Prof	ELA Pct Prof	Math Pct Prof
68.4	59.6	81.5	57.4	0.0	0.0	0.0	0.0
0.0	0.0	0.0	0.0	70.8	41.7	77.8	43.6
0.0	0.0	0.0	0.0	0.0	0.0	0.0	0.0
94.4	72.2	0.0	0.0	0.0	0.0	0.0	0.0
0.0	0.0	0.0	0.0	69.3	42.9	73.5	36.3
77.3	51.4	71.7	56.9	0.0	0.0	0.0	0.0
0.0	0.0	0.0	0.0	0.0	0.0	0.0	0.0
0.0	0.0	0.0	0.0	82.3	38.2	66.7	5.6
57.7	42.3	77.3	63.6	0.0	0.0	0.0	0.0
0.0	0.0	0.0	0.0	64.7	44.6	68.1	30.2
0.0	0.0	0.0	0.0	0.0	0.0	0.0	0.0
69.2	46.1	78.8	43.8	79.2	41.7	84.2	52.6
0.0	0.0	0.0	0.0	0.0	0.0	0.0	0.0
76.5	57.0	72.6	59.0	0.0	0.0	0.0	0.0
0.0	0.0	0.0	0.0	78.0	56.0	77.8	37.8
86.2	77.6	90.2	90.2	97.4	61.5	92.3	64.1
0.0	0.0	0.0	0.0	62.0	33.7	63.2	36.2
72.4	65.1	71.2	44.2	0.0	0.0	0.0	0.0
81.0	76.2	83.3	75.0	0.0	0.0	0.0	0.0
0.0	0.0	0.0	0.0	0.0	0.0	0.0	0.0
0.0	0.0	0.0	0.0	69.7	49.4	75.1	40.3
0.0	0.0	0.0	0.0	0.0	0.0	0.0	0.0
0.0	0.0	0.0	0.0	0.0	0.0	0.0	0.0
0.0	0.0	0.0	0.0	0.0	0.0	0.0	0.0
80.1	67.2	82.9	67.6	0.0	0.0	0.0	0.0
0.0	0.0	0.0	0.0	85.9	74.7	90.8	69.1
0.0	0.0	0.0	0.0	0.0	0.0	0.0	0.0

School Name	District Name	County Name	Zip Code	Median Home Value (k)	School Level
Van Arsdale Elementary School	Jefferson County R-1	Jefferson	80005	330400	1-Primary
West Woods Elementary School	Jefferson County R-1	Jefferson	80007	519900	1-Primary
Ryan Elementary School	Jefferson County R-1	Jefferson	80020	280800	1-Primary
Lukas Elementary School	Jefferson County R-1	Jefferson	80021	266200	1-Primary
Semper Elementary School	Jefferson County R-1	Jefferson	80021	266200	1-Primary
Standley Lake High School	Jefferson County R-1	Jefferson	80021	266200	3-High
Wayne Carle Middle School	Jefferson County R-1	Jefferson	80021	266200	2-Middle
Prospect Valley Elementary School	Jefferson County R-1	Jefferson	80033	296700	1-Primary
Blue Heron Elementary School	Jefferson County R-1	Jefferson	80123	306700	1-Primary
Columbine High School	Jefferson County R-1	Jefferson	80123	306700	3-High
Governor's Ranch Elementary School	Jefferson County R-1	Jefferson	80123	306700	1-Primary
Leawood Elementary School	Jefferson County R-1	Jefferson	80123	306700	1-Primary
Bradford Intermediate School	Jefferson County R-1	Jefferson	80127	359300	2-Middle
Bradford Primary School	Jefferson County R-1	Jefferson	80127	359300	1-Primary
Chatfield High School	Jefferson County R-1	Jefferson	80127	359300	3-High
Dakota Ridge Senior High School	Jefferson County R-1	Jefferson	80127	359300	3-High
Mount Carbon Elementary School	Jefferson County R-1	Jefferson	80127	359300	1-Primary
Powderhorn Elementary School	Jefferson County R-1	Jefferson	80127	359300	1-Primary
Shaffer Elementary School	Jefferson County R-1	Jefferson	80127	359300	1-Primary
Summit Ridge Middle School	Jefferson County R-1	Jefferson	80127	359300	2-Middle
Ute Meadows Elementary School	Jefferson County R-1	Jefferson	80127	359300	1-Primary

			Grade 3		Grade 4	
Pct Soc Dis	ELA Prof < 50%	Math Prof < 50%	ELA Pct Prof	Math Pct Prof	ELA Pct Prof	Math Pct Prof
15.4	0	0	85.5	88.4	86.4	89.8
5.9	0	0	95.1	96.3	85.4	97.1
24.1	0	0	91.4	91.4	85.5	81.2
27.4	0	0	82.5	75.0	80.2	83.8
28.3	0	0	81.4	83.0	71.2	63.5
30.1	0	2	0.0	0.0	0.0	0.0
27.3	0	0	0.0	0.0	0.0	0.0
28.1	0	0	87.7	81.5	72.7	65.8
15.7	0	0	90.8	90.8	75.0	79.4
21.0	0	1	0.0	0.0	0.0	0.0
12.3	0	0	85.7	76.6	86.8	86.8
22.9	0	0	83.3	85.4	88.7	94.4
3.0	0	0	0.0	0.0	94.1	96.6
4.8	0	0	93.6	95.5	0.0	0.0
14.4	0	0	0.0	0.0	0.0	0.0
17.5	0	0	0.0	0.0	0.0	0.0
14.6	0	0	89.8	87.9	90.0	95.0
20.8	0	0	90.9	86.9	86.0	82.6
6.8	0	0	93.5	88.2	91.2	92.0
21.3	0	0	0.0	0.0	0.0	0.0
11.5	0	0	87.3	87.3	82.7	81.1

School Name	Grade 5		Grade 6	
	ELA Pct Prof	Math Pct Prof	ELA Pct Prof	Math Pct Prof
Van Arsdale Elementary School	77.8	72.8	87.7	76.9
West Woods Elementary School	92.2	87.2	95.8	93.8
Ryan Elementary School	88.9	81.9	89.6	83.1
Lukas Elementary School	91.4	79.0	87.5	69.8
Semper Elementary School	83.3	63.9	85.7	65.2
Standley Lake High School	0.0	0.0	0.0	0.0
Wayne Carle Middle School	0.0	0.0	0.0	0.0
Prospect Valley Elementary School	89.5	77.6	86.1	84.3
Blue Heron Elementary School	79.3	74.1	92.4	86.4
Columbine High School	0.0	0.0	0.0	0.0
Governor's Ranch Elementary School	83.1	71.8	83.0	76.3
Leawood Elementary School	86.4	74.6	92.2	79.7
Bradford Intermediate School	99.1	95.4	98.6	92.9
Bradford Primary School	0.0	0.0	0.0	0.0
Chatfield High School	0.0	0.0	0.0	0.0
Dakota Ridge Senior High School	0.0	0.0	0.0	0.0
Mount Carbon Elementary School	86.2	79.3	92.4	83.3
Powderhorn Elementary School	95.8	86.3	89.2	77.5
Shaffer Elementary School	90.3	84.5	0.0	0.0
Summit Ridge Middle School	0.0	0.0	0.0	0.0
Ute Meadows Elementary School	93.5	87.0	94.8	93.4

Grade 7		Grade 8		Grade 9		Grade 10	
ELA Pct Prof	Math Pct Prof	ELA Pct Prof	Math Pct Prof	ELA Pct Prof	Math Pct Prof	ELA Pct Prof	Math Pct Prof
0.0	0.0	0.0	0.0	0.0	0.0	0.0	0.0
0.0	0.0	0.0	0.0	0.0	0.0	0.0	0.0
0.0	0.0	0.0	0.0	0.0	0.0	0.0	0.0
0.0	0.0	0.0	0.0	0.0	0.0	0.0	0.0
0.0	0.0	0.0	0.0	0.0	0.0	0.0	0.0
0.0	0.0	0.0	0.0	68.4	45.2	74.2	41.3
83.1	71.6	74.4	59.2	0.0	0.0	0.0	0.0
0.0	0.0	0.0	0.0	0.0	0.0	0.0	0.0
0.0	0.0	0.0	0.0	0.0	0.0	0.0	0.0
0.0	0.0	0.0	0.0	74.6	51.4	75.1	39.5
0.0	0.0	0.0	0.0	0.0	0.0	0.0	0.0
0.0	0.0	0.0	0.0	0.0	0.0	0.0	0.0
0.0	0.0	0.0	0.0	0.0	0.0	0.0	0.0
0.0	0.0	0.0	0.0	0.0	0.0	0.0	0.0
0.0	0.0	0.0	0.0	80.0	64.2	79.0	52.6
0.0	0.0	0.0	0.0	82.8	61.3	82.7	52.2
0.0	0.0	0.0	0.0	0.0	0.0	0.0	0.0
0.0	0.0	0.0	0.0	0.0	0.0	0.0	0.0
0.0	0.0	0.0	0.0	0.0	0.0	0.0	0.0
84.9	69.8	83.9	66.4	0.0	0.0	0.0	0.0
0.0	0.0	0.0	0.0	0.0	0.0	0.0	0.0

School Name	District Name	County Name	Zip Code	Median Home Value (k)	School Level
Westridge Elementary School	Jefferson County R-1	Jefferson	80127	359300	1-Primary
Coronado Elementary School	Jefferson County R-1	Jefferson	80128	302500	1-Primary
Deer Creek Middle School	Jefferson County R-1	Jefferson	80128	302500	2-Middle
Falcon Bluffs Middle School	Jefferson County R-1	Jefferson	80128	302500	2-Middle
Ken Caryl Middle School	Jefferson County R-1	Jefferson	80128	302500	2-Middle
Mortensen Elementary School	Jefferson County R-1	Jefferson	80128	302500	1-Primary
Normandy Elementary School	Jefferson County R-1	Jefferson	80128	302500	1-Primary
Stony Creek Elementary School	Jefferson County R-1	Jefferson	80128	302500	1-Primary
Lakewood High School	Jefferson County R-1	Jefferson	80215	349100	3-High
Dennison Elementary School	Jefferson County R-1	Jefferson	80226	280200	1-Primary
Jeffco's 21st Century Virtual Academy	Jefferson County R-1	Jefferson	80226	280200	3-High
Devinny Elementary School	Jefferson County R-1	Jefferson	80228	330100	1-Primary
Dunstan Middle School	Jefferson County R-1	Jefferson	80228	330100	2-Middle
Green Mountain High School	Jefferson County R-1	Jefferson	80228	330100	3-High
Hutchinson Elementary School	Jefferson County R-1	Jefferson	80228	330100	1-Primary
Rooney Ranch Elementary School	Jefferson County R-1	Jefferson	80228	330100	1-Primary
Kendrick Lakes Elementary School	Jefferson County R-1	Jefferson	80232	266700	1-Primary
D'evelyn Junior/Senior High School	Jefferson County R-1	Jefferson	80235	245900	3-High
Golden High School	Jefferson County R-1	Jefferson	80401	416600	3-High
Kyffin Elementary School	Jefferson County R-1	Jefferson	80401	416600	1-Primary
Manning Options School	Jefferson County R-1	Jefferson	80401	416600	2-Middle

			Grade 3		Grade 4	
Pct Soc Dis	ELA Prof < 50%	Math Prof < 50%	ELA Pct Prof	Math Pct Prof	ELA Pct Prof	Math Pct Prof
18.3	0	0	89.8	78.4	77.9	82.3
17.9	0	0	86.6	76.8	92.4	92.4
15.3	0	0	0.0	0.0	0.0	0.0
17.9	0	0	0.0	0.0	0.0	0.0
24.4	0	0	0.0	0.0	0.0	0.0
22.8	0	0	93.1	86.2	88.6	85.7
12.2	0	0	92.0	86.4	85.7	86.9
27.0	0	0	79.5	85.3	71.2	71.2
31.8	0	1	0.0	0.0	0.0	0.0
9.1	0	0	96.6	93.2	95.6	97.8
27.9	0	3	0.0	0.0	0.0	0.0
15.2	0	0	92.0	88.6	86.6	89.0
28.7	0	0	0.0	0.0	0.0	0.0
23.6	0	2	0.0	0.0	0.0	0.0
14.7	0	0	80.0	89.1	86.8	84.2
13.8	0	0	89.0	78.0	72.1	72.1
31.3	0	0	88.1	88.1	76.0	73.3
7.3	0	0	0.0	0.0	0.0	0.0
26.9	0	2	0.0	0.0	0.0	0.0
13.1	0	0	83.3	82.3	80.0	85.9
8.5	0	0	0.0	0.0	0.0	0.0

	Grade 5		Grade 6	
School Name	ELA Pct Prof	Math Pct Prof	ELA Pct Prof	Math Pct Prof
Westridge Elementary School	88.3	74.0	89.8	69.5
Coronado Elementary School	77.2	67.3	97.7	84.1
Deer Creek Middle School	0.0	0.0	0.0	0.0
Falcon Bluffs Middle School	0.0	0.0	92.3	77.5
Ken Caryl Middle School	0.0	0.0	0.0	0.0
Mortensen Elementary School	84.1	72.7	82.8	65.5
Normandy Elementary School	85.4	88.9	89.7	78.2
Stony Creek Elementary School	73.0	68.9	84.8	71.2
Lakewood High School	0.0	0.0	0.0	0.0
Dennison Elementary School	98.9	98.9	100.0	100.0
Jeffco's 21st Century Virtual Academy	0.0	0.0	0.0	0.0
Devinny Elementary School	97.3	84.0	92.5	88.2
Dunstan Middle School	0.0	0.0	0.0	0.0
Green Mountain High School	0.0	0.0	0.0	0.0
Hutchinson Elementary School	82.3	65.1	92.7	82.3
Rooney Ranch Elementary School	86.2	84.9	85.1	71.6
Kendrick Lakes Elementary School	80.4	87.0	84.3	66.7
D'evelyn Junior/Senior High School	0.0	0.0	0.0	0.0
Golden High School	0.0	0.0	0.0	0.0
Kyffin Elementary School	88.6	71.4	94.0	84.3
Manning Options School	0.0	0.0	0.0	0.0

Grade 7		Grade 8		Grade 9		Grade 10	
ELA Pct Prof	Math Pct Prof	ELA Pct Prof	Math Pct Prof	ELA Pct Prof	Math Pct Prof	ELA Pct Prof	Math Pct Prof
0.0	0.0	0.0	0.0	0.0	0.0	0.0	0.0
0.0	0.0	0.0	0.0	0.0	0.0	0.0	0.0
89.8	82.0	90.2	78.4	0.0	0.0	0.0	0.0
82.0	74.8	79.8	67.4	0.0	0.0	0.0	0.0
79.7	67.8	82.3	61.8	0.0	0.0	0.0	0.0
0.0	0.0	0.0	0.0	0.0	0.0	0.0	0.0
0.0	0.0	0.0	0.0	0.0	0.0	0.0	0.0
0.0	0.0	0.0	0.0	0.0	0.0	0.0	0.0
0.0	0.0	0.0	0.0	72.9	55.7	73.5	44.1
0.0	0.0	0.0	0.0	0.0	0.0	0.0	0.0
81.0	55.0	54.8	32.3	76.7	25.8	62.9	17.5
0.0	0.0	0.0	0.0	0.0	0.0	0.0	0.0
82.6	69.6	79.7	65.8	0.0	0.0	0.0	0.0
0.0	0.0	0.0	0.0	74.1	49.8	78.1	41.6
0.0	0.0	0.0	0.0	0.0	0.0	0.0	0.0
0.0	0.0	0.0	0.0	0.0	0.0	0.0	0.0
0.0	0.0	0.0	0.0	0.0	0.0	0.0	0.0
95.4	91.2	97.5	97.0	97.0	91.0	96.4	92.2
0.0	0.0	0.0	0.0	70.5	46.8	77.0	41.5
0.0	0.0	0.0	0.0	0.0	0.0	0.0	0.0
95.9	96.8	96.4	94.2	0.0	0.0	0.0	0.0

School Name	District Name	County Name	Zip Code	Median Home Value (k)	School Level
Maple Grove Elementary School	Jefferson County R-1	Jefferson	80401	416600	1-Primary
Ralston Elementary School	Jefferson County R-1	Jefferson	80401	416600	1-Primary
Coal Creek Canyon K-8 Elementary School	Jefferson County R-1	Jefferson	80403	418400	1-Primary
Fairmount Elementary School	Jefferson County R-1	Jefferson	80403	418400	1-Primary
Mitchell Elementary School	Jefferson County R-1	Jefferson	80403	418400	1-Primary
Conifer Senior High School	Jefferson County R-1	Jefferson	80433	383400	3-High
West Jefferson Elementary School	Jefferson County R-1	Jefferson	80433	383400	1-Primary
West Jefferson Middle School	Jefferson County R-1	Jefferson	80433	383400	2-Middle
Bergen Valley Intermediate School	Jefferson County R-1	Jefferson	80439	457000	1-Primary
Evergreen High School	Jefferson County R-1	Jefferson	80439	457000	3-High
Evergreen Middle School	Jefferson County R-1	Jefferson	80439	457000	2-Middle
Marshdale Elementary School	Jefferson County R-1	Jefferson	80439	457000	1-Primary
Wilmot Elementary School	Jefferson County R-1	Jefferson	80439	457000	1-Primary
Parmalee Elementary School	Jefferson County R-1	Jefferson	80454	337300	1-Primary
Red Rocks Elementary School	Jefferson County R-1	Jefferson	80465	308300	1-Primary
Elk Creek Elementary School	Jefferson County R-1	Jefferson	80470	312800	1-Primary
Bayfield High School	Bayfield 10 Jt-R	La Plata	81122	247800	3-High
Durango High School	Durango 9-R	La Plata	81301	386200	3-High
Miller Middle School	Durango 9-R	La Plata	81301	386200	2-Middle
Riverview Elementary School	Durango 9-R	La Plata	81301	386200	1-Primary
Estes Park High School	Estes Park R-3	Larimer	80517	355000	3-High
Estes Park Middle School	Estes Park R-3	Larimer	80517	355000	2-Middle
Bennett Elementary School	Poudre R-1	Larimer	80521	258300	1-Primary
Dunn Elementary School	Poudre R-1	Larimer	80525	300900	1-Primary
Fort Collins High School	Poudre R-1	Larimer	80525	300900	3-High

Pct Soc Dis	ELA Prof < 50%	Math Prof < 50%	Grade 3		Grade 4	
			ELA Pct Prof	Math Pct Prof	ELA Pct Prof	Math Pct Prof
9.9	0	0	80.0	76.4	92.2	90.2
4.7	0	0	92.7	95.6	93.8	95.8
24.1	0	0	0.0	0.0	88.9	81.5
7.0	0	0	82.4	80.2	92.3	94.5
15.7	0	0	92.0	88.5	87.0	87.0
14.6	0	0	0.0	0.0	0.0	0.0
16.0	0	0	83.3	71.4	91.7	86.1
17.4	0	0	0.0	0.0	0.0	0.0
6.7	0	0	96.3	98.2	94.0	90.4
9.9	0	0	0.0	0.0	0.0	0.0
11.6	0	0	0.0	0.0	0.0	0.0
10.4	0	0	87.8	89.8	94.4	83.3
16.0	0	0	95.6	97.8	85.5	87.3
19.2	0	0	95.5	95.3	92.2	92.2
11.3	0	0	88.2	80.4	97.7	93.0
25.2	0	0	98.1	90.4	83.3	81.2
26.7	0	2	0.0	0.0	0.0	0.0
23.2	0	2	0.0	0.0	0.0	0.0
28.6	0	1	0.0	0.0	0.0	0.0
18.6	0	0	88.5	83.0	85.9	78.9
29.2	0	2	0.0	0.0	0.0	0.0
32.8	0	2	0.0	0.0	0.0	0.0
24.9	0	0	87.8	86.6	85.9	84.0
28.4	0	0	84.6	85.9	83.6	87.7
29.4	0	2	0.0	0.0	0.0	0.0

	Grade 5		Grade 6	
School Name	ELA Pct Prof	Math Pct Prof	ELA Pct Prof	Math Pct Prof
Maple Grove Elementary School	85.9	90.6	94.5	85.5
Ralston Elementary School	92.1	92.1	96.5	89.7
Coal Creek Canyon K-8 Elementary School	68.8	62.5	0.0	0.0
Fairmount Elementary School	90.0	86.4	86.5	80.7
Mitchell Elementary School	88.9	84.3	0.0	0.0
Conifer Senior High School	0.0	0.0	0.0	0.0
West Jefferson Elementary School	90.2	78.7	0.0	0.0
West Jefferson Middle School	0.0	0.0	87.0	75.7
Bergen Valley Intermediate School	95.8	88.8	0.0	0.0
Evergreen High School	0.0	0.0	0.0	0.0
Evergreen Middle School	0.0	0.0	94.8	88.2
Marshdale Elementary School	94.8	96.5	0.0	0.0
Wilmot Elementary School	86.0	84.0	0.0	0.0
Parmalee Elementary School	93.3	89.1	0.0	0.0
Red Rocks Elementary School	95.3	86.0	94.3	80.0
Elk Creek Elementary School	94.8	84.5	0.0	0.0
Bayfield High School	0.0	0.0	0.0	0.0
Durango High School	0.0	0.0	0.0	0.0
Miller Middle School	0.0	0.0	75.3	63.1
Riverview Elementary School	81.8	69.7	0.0	0.0
Estes Park High School	0.0	0.0	0.0	0.0
Estes Park Middle School	0.0	0.0	75.0	64.7
Bennett Elementary School	83.0	83.0	0.0	0.0
Dunn Elementary School	90.6	89.1	0.0	0.0
Fort Collins High School	0.0	0.0	0.0	0.0

Grade 7		Grade 8		Grade 9		Grade 10	
ELA Pct Prof	Math Pct Prof	ELA Pct Prof	Math Pct Prof	ELA Pct Prof	Math Pct Prof	ELA Pct Prof	Math Pct Prof
0.0	0.0	0.0	0.0	0.0	0.0	0.0	0.0
0.0	0.0	0.0	0.0	0.0	0.0	0.0	0.0
88.9	61.1	95.0	85.0	0.0	0.0	0.0	0.0
0.0	0.0	0.0	0.0	0.0	0.0	0.0	0.0
0.0	0.0	0.0	0.0	0.0	0.0	0.0	0.0
0.0	0.0	0.0	0.0	81.9	63.6	83.2	57.0
0.0	0.0	0.0	0.0	0.0	0.0	0.0	0.0
87.0	75.1	82.1	66.1	0.0	0.0	0.0	0.0
0.0	0.0	0.0	0.0	0.0	0.0	0.0	0.0
0.0	0.0	0.0	0.0	88.3	77.7	89.6	63.8
92.5	89.0	92.6	82.1	0.0	0.0	0.0	0.0
0.0	0.0	0.0	0.0	0.0	0.0	0.0	0.0
0.0	0.0	0.0	0.0	0.0	0.0	0.0	0.0
0.0	0.0	0.0	0.0	0.0	0.0	0.0	0.0
0.0	0.0	0.0	0.0	0.0	0.0	0.0	0.0
0.0	0.0	0.0	0.0	0.0	0.0	0.0	0.0
0.0	0.0	0.0	0.0	68.4	39.0	75.6	41.5
0.0	0.0	0.0	0.0	76.5	46.6	80.7	39.6
75.6	54.2	75.9	49.2	0.0	0.0	0.0	0.0
0.0	0.0	0.0	0.0	0.0	0.0	0.0	0.0
0.0	0.0	0.0	0.0	79.8	48.8	78.5	47.7
61.7	42.0	58.8	38.8	0.0	0.0	0.0	0.0
0.0	0.0	0.0	0.0	0.0	0.0	0.0	0.0
0.0	0.0	0.0	0.0	0.0	0.0	0.0	0.0
0.0	0.0	0.0	0.0	68.4	47.2	72.4	39.6

School Name	District Name	County Name	Zip Code	Median Home Value (k)	School Level
Kruse Elementary School	Poudre R-1	Larimer	80525	300900	1-Primary
Shepardson Elementary School	Poudre R-1	Larimer	80525	300900	1-Primary
Werner Elementary School	Poudre R-1	Larimer	80525	300900	1-Primary
Johnson Elementary School	Poudre R-1	Larimer	80526	272400	1-Primary
Mcgraw Elementary School	Poudre R-1	Larimer	80526	272400	1-Primary
Rocky Mountain High School	Poudre R-1	Larimer	80526	272400	3-High
Webber Middle School	Poudre R-1	Larimer	80526	272400	2-Middle
Bacon Elementary School	Poudre R-1	Larimer	80528	376000	1-Primary
Fossil Ridge High School	Poudre R-1	Larimer	80528	376000	3-High
Kinard Core Knowledge Middle School	Poudre R-1	Larimer	80528	376000	2-Middle
Preston Middle School	Poudre R-1	Larimer	80528	376000	2-Middle
Traut Core Elementary School	Poudre R-1	Larimer	80528	376000	1-Primary
Zach Elementary School	Poudre R-1	Larimer	80528	376000	1-Primary
Bethke Elementary School	Poudre R-1	Larimer	80547	402000	1-Primary
Berthoud Elementary School	Thompson R2-J	Larimer	80513	328900	1-Primary
Berthoud High School	Thompson R2-J	Larimer	80513	328900	3-High
Turner Middle School	Thompson R2-J	Larimer	80513	328900	2-Middle
Coyote Ridge Elementary School	Thompson R2-J	Larimer	80525	300900	1-Primary
Mountain View High School	Thompson R2-J	Larimer	80537	239900	3-High
Namaqua Elementary School	Thompson R2-J	Larimer	80537	239900	1-Primary
Thompson Valley High School	Thompson R2-J	Larimer	80537	239900	3-High
Big Thompson Elementary School	Thompson R2-J	Larimer	80538	252200	1-Primary
Centennial Elementary School	Thompson R2-J	Larimer	80538	252200	1-Primary
Loveland High School	Thompson R2-J	Larimer	80538	252200	3-High
Ponderosa Elementary	Thompson R2-J	Larimer	80538	252200	1-Primary
Branson School Online	Branson Reorganized 82	Las Animas	81027	87500	4-Other
Merino Junior Senior High School	Buffalo Re-4j	Logan	80741	151000	3-High
Peetz Elementary School	Plateau Re-5	Logan	80747	89400	1-Primary
Peetz Junior-Senior High School	Plateau Re-5	Logan	80747	89400	3-High
New Emerson School At Columbus	Mesa County Valley 51	Mesa	81503	161700	1-Primary
Appleton Elementary School	Mesa County Valley 51	Mesa	81505	219300	1-Primary
Broadway Elementary School	Mesa County Valley 51	Mesa	81507	282900	1-Primary

Pct Soc Dis	ELA Prof < 50%	Math Prof < 50%	Grade 3		Grade 4	
			ELA Pct Prof	Math Pct Prof	ELA Pct Prof	Math Pct Prof
23.8	0	0	89.4	94.7	87.2	88.3
23.2	0	0	75.4	72.9	70.0	75.6
10.9	0	0	92.7	89.6	94.6	92.5
27.4	0	0	74.6	80.3	66.2	76.5
15.8	0	0	84.0	86.1	87.5	90.0
26.8	0	2	0.0	0.0	0.0	0.0
28.5	0	0	0.0	0.0	0.0	0.0
16.8	0	0	87.2	81.4	80.5	81.7
8.9	0	0	0.0	0.0	0.0	0.0
7.0	0	0	0.0	0.0	0.0	0.0
15.1	0	0	0.0	0.0	0.0	0.0
8.3	0	0	93.3	90.7	94.7	94.7
3.1	0	0	98.2	100.0	94.6	96.2
4.8	0	0	97.6	98.8	96.7	97.8
21.6	0	0	90.9	92.4	95.1	98.4
18.7	0	1	0.0	0.0	0.0	0.0
23.4	0	0	0.0	0.0	0.0	0.0
14.7	0	0	90.9	90.9	96.2	86.8
31.9	0	2	0.0	0.0	0.0	0.0
27.1	0	0	82.5	79.0	88.1	88.1
27.5	0	2	0.0	0.0	0.0	0.0
24.6	0	0	80.0	85.7	80.0	80.0
25.8	0	0	83.1	83.6	79.3	85.4
29.8	0	2	0.0	0.0	0.0	0.0
25.8	0	0	78.9	72.9	84.8	80.3
14.0	0	3	93.1	78.6	58.8	52.9
32.1	0	3	0.0	0.0	0.0	0.0
32.3	0	0	0.0	0.0	0.0	0.0
29.6	0	1	0.0	0.0	0.0	0.0
14.0	0	0	95.7	95.7	90.9	100.0
28.9	0	0	61.5	72.5	69.2	80.0
21.8	0	0	78.3	73.9	64.1	71.8

School Name	Grade 5		Grade 6	
	ELA Pct Prof	Math Pct Prof	ELA Pct Prof	Math Pct Prof
Kruse Elementary School	87.8	85.7	0.0	0.0
Shepardson Elementary School	79.3	70.7	0.0	0.0
Werner Elementary School	87.0	87.9	0.0	0.0
Johnson Elementary School	85.5	85.5	0.0	0.0
Mcgraw Elementary School	83.6	89.0	0.0	0.0
Rocky Mountain High School	0.0	0.0	0.0	0.0
Webber Middle School	0.0	0.0	86.8	73.6
Bacon Elementary School	86.4	82.0	0.0	0.0
Fossil Ridge High School	0.0	0.0	0.0	0.0
Kinard Core Knowledge Middle School	0.0	0.0	93.9	88.2
Preston Middle School	0.0	0.0	90.1	85.7
Traut Core Elementary School	96.0	94.7	0.0	0.0
Zach Elementary School	96.7	89.9	0.0	0.0
Bethke Elementary School	90.3	95.7	0.0	0.0
Berthoud Elementary School	89.3	88.0	0.0	0.0
Berthoud High School	0.0	0.0	0.0	0.0
Turner Middle School	0.0	0.0	85.2	79.3
Coyote Ridge Elementary School	93.1	84.5	0.0	0.0
Mountain View High School	0.0	0.0	0.0	0.0
Namaqua Elementary School	76.8	60.7	0.0	0.0
Thompson Valley High School	0.0	0.0	0.0	0.0
Big Thompson Elementary School	80.8	80.8	0.0	0.0
Centennial Elementary School	82.6	72.5	0.0	0.0
Loveland High School	0.0	0.0	0.0	0.0
Ponderosa Elementary	90.2	80.4	0.0	0.0
Branson School Online	68.2	68.2	76.5	55.9
Merino Junior Senior High School	0.0	0.0	0.0	0.0
Peetz Elementary School	76.5	64.7	0.0	0.0
Peetz Junior-Senior High School	0.0	0.0	0.0	0.0
New Emerson School At Columbus	90.9	100.0	0.0	0.0
Appleton Elementary School	77.9	69.1	0.0	0.0
Broadway Elementary School	84.6	84.6	0.0	0.0

Grade 7		Grade 8		Grade 9		Grade 10	
ELA Pct Prof	Math Pct Prof	ELA Pct Prof	Math Pct Prof	ELA Pct Prof	Math Pct Prof	ELA Pct Prof	Math Pct Prof
0.0	0.0	0.0	0.0	0.0	0.0	0.0	0.0
0.0	0.0	0.0	0.0	0.0	0.0	0.0	0.0
0.0	0.0	0.0	0.0	0.0	0.0	0.0	0.0
0.0	0.0	0.0	0.0	0.0	0.0	0.0	0.0
0.0	0.0	0.0	0.0	0.0	0.0	0.0	0.0
0.0	0.0	0.0	0.0	72.8	47.3	79.1	43.2
74.8	63.7	80.5	66.4	0.0	0.0	0.0	0.0
0.0	0.0	0.0	0.0	0.0	0.0	0.0	0.0
0.0	0.0	0.0	0.0	89.4	62.5	86.9	57.4
92.3	83.8	93.9	82.9	0.0	0.0	0.0	0.0
88.7	79.3	86.7	81.8	0.0	0.0	0.0	0.0
0.0	0.0	0.0	0.0	0.0	0.0	0.0	0.0
0.0	0.0	0.0	0.0	0.0	0.0	0.0	0.0
0.0	0.0	0.0	0.0	0.0	0.0	0.0	0.0
0.0	0.0	0.0	0.0	0.0	0.0	0.0	0.0
0.0	0.0	0.0	0.0	84.2	49.1	91.4	58.6
84.8	74.6	80.4	69.3	0.0	0.0	0.0	0.0
0.0	0.0	0.0	0.0	0.0	0.0	0.0	0.0
0.0	0.0	0.0	0.0	65.0	26.1	70.5	23.7
0.0	0.0	0.0	0.0	0.0	0.0	0.0	0.0
0.0	0.0	0.0	0.0	66.3	38.7	68.4	26.3
0.0	0.0	0.0	0.0	0.0	0.0	0.0	0.0
0.0	0.0	0.0	0.0	0.0	0.0	0.0	0.0
0.0	0.0	0.0	0.0	67.4	38.4	76.1	44.3
0.0	0.0	0.0	0.0	0.0	0.0	0.0	0.0
75.0	56.2	77.5	37.5	76.3	23.7	90.0	22.5
57.1	66.7	72.0	48.0	71.4	39.3	90.0	43.3
0.0	0.0	0.0	0.0	0.0	0.0	0.0	0.0
88.2	72.2	72.2	50.0	0.0	0.0	90.0	52.4
0.0	0.0	0.0	0.0	0.0	0.0	0.0	0.0
0.0	0.0	0.0	0.0	0.0	0.0	0.0	0.0
0.0	0.0	0.0	0.0	0.0	0.0	0.0	0.0

School Name	District Name	County Name	Zip Code	Median Home Value (k)	School Level
Grande River Virtual Academy	Mesa County Valley 51	Mesa	81507	282900	
Redlands Middle School	Mesa County Valley 51	Mesa	81507	282900	2-Middle
Scenic Elementary School	Mesa County Valley 51	Mesa	81507	282900	1-Primary
Wingate Elementary School	Mesa County Valley 51	Mesa	81507	282900	1-Primary
Fruita 8/9 School	Mesa County Valley 51	Mesa	81521	201900	4-Other
Fruita Monument High School	Mesa County Valley 51	Mesa	81521	201900	3-High
Loma Elementary School	Mesa County Valley 51	Mesa	81524	365700	1-Primary
Plateau Valley Elementary School	Plateau Valley 50	Mesa	81624	222400	1-Primary
Plateau Valley High School	Plateau Valley 50	Mesa	81624	222400	3-High
Cottonwood Elementary School	Montrose County Re-1j	Montrose	81402	200200	1-Primary
Weldon Valley High School	Weldon Valley Re-20(J)	Morgan	80653	120500	3-High
Ouray Senior High School	Ouray R-1	Ouray	81427	450000	3-High
Ridgway High School	Ridgway R-2	Ouray	81432	444000	3-High
Deer Creek Elementary School	Platte Canyon 1	Park	80421	239000	1-Primary
Haxtun Elementary School	Haxtun Re-2j	Phillips	80731	116900	1-Primary
Haxtun High School	Haxtun Re-2j	Phillips	80731	116900	3-High
Aspen Elementary School	Aspen 1	Pitkin	81611	647100	1-Primary
Aspen High School	Aspen 1	Pitkin	81611	647100	3-High
Aspen Middle School	Aspen 1	Pitkin	81611	647100	2-Middle
Cedar Ridge Elementary School	Pueblo County 70	Pueblo	81007	174000	1-Primary
Prairie Winds Elementary School	Pueblo County 70	Pueblo	81007	174000	1-Primary
Pueblo West High School	Pueblo County 70	Pueblo	81007	174000	3-High
Sierra Vista Elementary School	Pueblo County 70	Pueblo	81007	174000	1-Primary
Sky View Middle School	Pueblo County 70	Pueblo	81007	174000	2-Middle
Meeker Elementary School	Meeker Re1	Rio Blanco	81641	241200	1-Primary
Meeker High School	Meeker Re1	Rio Blanco	81641	241200	3-High
Parkview Elementary School	Rangely Re-4	Rio Blanco	81648	168300	1-Primary
Rangely Junior/Senior High School	Rangely Re-4	Rio Blanco	81648	168300	4-Other
Sargent Junior High School	Sargent Re-33j	Rio Grande	81144	127000	2-Middle
Hayden High School	Hayden Re-1	Routt	81639	202500	3-High

	Pct Soc Dis	ELA Prof < 50%	Math Prof < 50%	Grade 3		Grade 4	
				ELA Pct Prof	Math Pct Prof	ELA Pct Prof	Math Pct Prof
	9.4	1	3	0.0	0.0	0.0	0.0
	23.4	0	0	0.0	0.0	0.0	0.0
	31.7	0	0	82.6	82.6	89.5	86.8
	18.7	0	0	78.8	87.9	72.6	75.0
	27.9	0	1	0.0	0.0	0.0	0.0
	24.3	0	1	0.0	0.0	0.0	0.0
	29.3	0	0	84.0	92.0	67.3	61.5
	31.2	0	0	65.5	65.5	61.3	54.8
	32.1	0	2	0.0	0.0	0.0	0.0
	32.5	0	0	79.2	79.5	80.6	83.3
	28.3	0	2	0.0	0.0	0.0	0.0
	32.1	0	0	0.0	0.0	0.0	0.0
	23.8	0	1	0.0	0.0	0.0	0.0
	32.0	0	0	89.1	76.2	81.8	80.5
	31.9	0	1	63.6	87.0	58.3	70.8
	29.2	0	2	0.0	0.0	0.0	0.0
	6.4	0	0	91.6	80.6	88.8	86.8
	6.6	0	0	0.0	0.0	0.0	0.0
	9.2	0	0	0.0	0.0	0.0	0.0
	22.0	0	0	72.1	74.6	72.2	80.0
	31.8	0	0	77.6	82.7	64.5	68.4
	32.5	0	2	0.0	0.0	0.0	0.0
	32.6	0	0	68.1	76.5	83.8	77.5
	28.9	0	1	0.0	0.0	0.0	0.0
	26.2	0	0	81.8	81.8	82.7	84.3
	25.6	0	2	0.0	0.0	0.0	0.0
	21.0	0	1	75.0	62.5	51.4	66.7
	25.8	0	4	0.0	0.0	0.0	0.0
	29.1	0	1	0.0	0.0	0.0	0.0
	24.8	0	2	0.0	0.0	0.0	0.0

School Name	Grade 5		Grade 6	
	ELA Pct Prof	Math Pct Prof	ELA Pct Prof	Math Pct Prof
Grande River Virtual Academy	0.0	0.0	68.8	25.0
Redlands Middle School	0.0	0.0	79.6	73.0
Scenic Elementary School	89.1	76.1	0.0	0.0
Wingate Elementary School	72.8	68.5	0.0	0.0
Fruita 8/9 School	0.0	0.0	0.0	0.0
Fruita Monument High School	0.0	0.0	0.0	0.0
Loma Elementary School	71.1	60.0	0.0	0.0
Plateau Valley Elementary School	70.8	58.3	0.0	0.0
Plateau Valley High School	0.0	0.0	0.0	0.0
Cottonwood Elementary School	69.9	67.1	0.0	0.0
Weldon Valley High School	0.0	0.0	0.0	0.0
Ouray Senior High School	0.0	0.0	0.0	0.0
Ridgway High School	0.0	0.0	0.0	0.0
Deer Creek Elementary School	84.3	74.3	0.0	0.0
Haxtun Elementary School	68.0	56.0	70.6	47.1
Haxtun High School	0.0	0.0	0.0	0.0
Aspen Elementary School	0.0	0.0	0.0	0.0
Aspen High School	0.0	0.0	0.0	0.0
Aspen Middle School	86.4	75.5	83.3	72.6
Cedar Ridge Elementary School	76.2	75.0	0.0	0.0
Prairie Winds Elementary School	76.6	70.1	0.0	0.0
Pueblo West High School	0.0	0.0	0.0	0.0
Sierra Vista Elementary School	75.3	68.5	0.0	0.0
Sky View Middle School	0.0	0.0	78.3	63.3
Meeker Elementary School	51.2	53.5	0.0	0.0
Meeker High School	0.0	0.0	0.0	0.0
Parkview Elementary School	56.1	41.5	0.0	0.0
Rangely Junior/Senior High School	0.0	0.0	72.4	65.5
Sargent Junior High School	0.0	0.0	0.0	0.0
Hayden High School	0.0	0.0	0.0	0.0

Grade 7		Grade 8		Grade 9		Grade 10	
ELA Pct Prof	Math Pct Prof	ELA Pct Prof	Math Pct Prof	ELA Pct Prof	Math Pct Prof	ELA Pct Prof	Math Pct Prof
0.0	0.0	0.0	0.0	50.0	4.5	66.7	19.1
79.0	72.8	76.8	63.7	0.0	0.0	0.0	0.0
0.0	0.0	0.0	0.0	0.0	0.0	0.0	0.0
0.0	0.0	0.0	0.0	0.0	0.0	0.0	0.0
0.0	0.0	71.3	57.1	76.5	41.7	0.0	0.0
0.0	0.0	0.0	0.0	0.0	0.0	78.7	30.4
0.0	0.0	0.0	0.0	0.0	0.0	0.0	0.0
0.0	0.0	0.0	0.0	0.0	0.0	0.0	0.0
0.0	0.0	0.0	0.0	75.0	31.6	85.0	25.0
0.0	0.0	0.0	0.0	0.0	0.0	0.0	0.0
0.0	0.0	0.0	0.0	82.3	47.1	94.1	35.3
0.0	0.0	0.0	0.0	0.0	0.0	82.3	64.7
0.0	0.0	0.0	0.0	82.8	55.2	89.3	50.0
0.0	0.0	0.0	0.0	0.0	0.0	0.0	0.0
79.0	52.6	60.9	56.5	0.0	0.0	0.0	0.0
0.0	0.0	0.0	0.0	54.5	27.3	76.0	40.0
0.0	0.0	0.0	0.0	0.0	0.0	0.0	0.0
0.0	0.0	0.0	0.0	84.9	65.1	88.8	57.2
88.3	72.9	86.2	72.2	0.0	0.0	0.0	0.0
0.0	0.0	0.0	0.0	0.0	0.0	0.0	0.0
0.0	0.0	0.0	0.0	0.0	0.0	0.0	0.0
0.0	0.0	0.0	0.0	75.2	35.4	79.1	24.9
0.0	0.0	0.0	0.0	0.0	0.0	0.0	0.0
77.0	49.0	71.7	51.8	0.0	0.0	0.0	0.0
0.0	0.0	0.0	0.0	0.0	0.0	0.0	0.0
0.0	0.0	0.0	0.0	74.0	38.0	65.8	23.7
0.0	0.0	0.0	0.0	0.0	0.0	0.0	0.0
66.7	33.3	70.0	36.7	64.5	32.3	91.7	33.3
75.8	48.5	68.2	54.5	0.0	0.0	0.0	0.0
0.0	0.0	0.0	0.0	67.9	35.7	90.5	14.3

School Name	District Name	County Name	Zip Code	Median Home Value (k)	School Level
Soroco High School	South Routt Re 3	Routt	80467	178500	3-High
Soda Creek Elementary School	Steamboat Springs Re-2	Routt	80487	391800	1-Primary
Steamboat Springs High School	Steamboat Springs Re-2	Routt	80487	391800	3-High
Steamboat Springs Middle School	Steamboat Springs Re-2	Routt	80487	391800	2-Middle
Strawberry Park Elementary School	Steamboat Springs Re-2	Routt	80487	391800	1-Primary
Telluride Elementary School	Telluride R-1	San Miguel	81435	748900	1-Primary
Telluride High School	Telluride R-1	San Miguel	81435	748900	3-High
Telluride Middle School	Telluride R-1	San Miguel	81435	748900	2-Middle
Breckenridge Elementary School	Summit Re-1	Summit	80424	499600	1-Primary
Upper Blue Elementary School	Summit Re-1	Summit	80424	499600	1-Primary
Summit Cove Elementary School	Summit Re-1	Summit	80435	388500	1-Primary
Frisco Elementary School	Summit Re-1	Summit	80443	525400	1-Primary
Summit High School	Summit Re-1	Summit	80443	525400	3-High
Columbine Elementary School	Woodland Park Re-2	Teller	80863	255400	1-Primary
Woodland Park High School	Woodland Park Re-2	Teller	80863	255400	3-High
Akron High School	Akron R-1	Washington	80720	109000	3-High
Eaton High School	Eaton Re-2	Weld	80615	242000	3-High
Letford Elementary School	Johnstown-Milliken Re-5j	Weld	80534	272500	1-Primary
Pioneer Ridge Elementary School	Johnstown-Milliken Re-5j	Weld	80534	272500	1-Primary
Platte Valley High School	Platte Valley Re-7	Weld	80644	199300	3-High
Prairie Junior-Senior High School	Prairie Re-11	Weld	80742	97900	3-High
Grandview Elementary School	Windsor Re-4	Weld	80550	295700	1-Primary
Mountain View Elementary School	Windsor Re-4	Weld	80550	295700	1-Primary
Range View Elementary	Windsor Re-4	Weld	80550	295700	1-Primary
Severance Middle School	Windsor Re-4	Weld	80550	295700	2-Middle
Skyview Elementary School	Windsor Re-4	Weld	80550	295700	1-Primary
Windsor High School	Windsor Re-4	Weld	80550	295700	3-High
Windsor Middle School	Windsor Re-4	Weld	80550	295700	2-Middle

			Grade 3		Grade 4	
Pct Soc Dis	ELA Prof < 50%	Math Prof < 50%	ELA Pct Prof	Math Pct Prof	ELA Pct Prof	Math Pct Prof
27.2	0	2	0.0	0.0	0.0	0.0
16.0	0	0	76.4	85.4	94.2	85.4
16.5	0	0	0.0	0.0	0.0	0.0
18.6	0	0	0.0	0.0	0.0	0.0
20.4	0	0	91.8	90.7	79.6	84.7
25.5	0	0	71.9	82.5	72.5	72.5
24.1	0	1	0.0	0.0	0.0	0.0
30.8	0	0	0.0	0.0	0.0	0.0
13.8	0	0	88.6	94.3	79.5	90.9
31.1	0	0	88.7	76.9	93.9	91.2
26.8	0	0	85.3	77.1	79.1	90.5
17.4	0	0	92.3	97.4	75.8	90.9
21.6	0	1	0.0	0.0	0.0	0.0
23.0	0	0	82.1	79.7	63.2	71.9
29.7	0	2	0.0	0.0	0.0	0.0
31.1	0	2	0.0	0.0	0.0	0.0
26.6	0	2	0.0	0.0	0.0	0.0
32.3	0	0	81.0	84.1	76.6	71.9
16.9	0	0	75.7	83.9	80.2	89.0
28.6	0	2	0.0	0.0	0.0	0.0
21.9	0	0	0.0	0.0	0.0	0.0
22.2	0	0	90.7	80.0	80.0	84.6
23.5	0	0	79.4	82.9	82.5	83.5
18.9	0	0	70.2	84.0	77.5	79.0
18.6	0	0	0.0	0.0	0.0	0.0
26.3	0	0	84.0	87.8	82.3	90.3
16.3	0	2	0.0	0.0	0.0	0.0
25.2	0	0	0.0	0.0	0.0	0.0

School Name	Grade 5		Grade 6	
	ELA Pct Prof	Math Pct Prof	ELA Pct Prof	Math Pct Prof
Soroco High School	0.0	0.0	0.0	0.0
Soda Creek Elementary School	89.8	83.3	0.0	0.0
Steamboat Springs High School	0.0	0.0	0.0	0.0
Steamboat Springs Middle School	0.0	0.0	91.5	87.0
Strawberry Park Elementary School	96.7	93.5	0.0	0.0
Telluride Elementary School	92.2	86.3	78.1	64.4
Telluride High School	0.0	0.0	0.0	0.0
Telluride Middle School	0.0	0.0	0.0	0.0
Breckenridge Elementary School	91.2	76.5	0.0	0.0
Upper Blue Elementary School	82.9	71.4	0.0	0.0
Summit Cove Elementary School	83.6	75.9	0.0	0.0
Frisco Elementary School	86.8	84.2	0.0	0.0
Summit High School	0.0	0.0	0.0	0.0
Columbine Elementary School	84.5	73.2	0.0	0.0
Woodland Park High School	0.0	0.0	0.0	0.0
Akron High School	0.0	0.0	0.0	0.0
Eaton High School	0.0	0.0	0.0	0.0
Letford Elementary School	76.9	68.3	0.0	0.0
Pioneer Ridge Elementary School	78.6	70.4	0.0	0.0
Platte Valley High School	0.0	0.0	0.0	0.0
Prairie Junior-Senior High School	0.0	0.0	0.0	0.0
Grandview Elementary School	81.7	83.3	0.0	0.0
Mountain View Elementary School	73.0	62.0	0.0	0.0
Range View Elementary	86.3	83.2	0.0	0.0
Severance Middle School	0.0	0.0	76.2	77.5
Skyview Elementary School	81.7	69.5	0.0	0.0
Windsor High School	0.0	0.0	0.0	0.0
Windsor Middle School	0.0	0.0	76.8	75.7

Grade 7		Grade 8		Grade 9		Grade 10	
ELA Pct Prof	Math Pct Prof	ELA Pct Prof	Math Pct Prof	ELA Pct Prof	Math Pct Prof	ELA Pct Prof	Math Pct Prof
0.0	0.0	0.0	0.0	60.9	30.4	61.5	30.8
0.0	0.0	0.0	0.0	0.0	0.0	0.0	0.0
0.0	0.0	0.0	0.0	83.7	69.1	94.7	56.7
82.7	80.8	84.2	80.5	0.0	0.0	0.0	0.0
0.0	0.0	0.0	0.0	0.0	0.0	0.0	0.0
0.0	0.0	0.0	0.0	0.0	0.0	0.0	0.0
0.0	0.0	0.0	0.0	85.0	53.3	81.8	45.5
89.1	79.7	80.0	65.2	0.0	0.0	0.0	0.0
0.0	0.0	0.0	0.0	0.0	0.0	0.0	0.0
0.0	0.0	0.0	0.0	0.0	0.0	0.0	0.0
0.0	0.0	0.0	0.0	0.0	0.0	0.0	0.0
0.0	0.0	0.0	0.0	0.0	0.0	0.0	0.0
0.0	0.0	0.0	0.0	69.5	53.3	81.9	44.2
0.0	0.0	0.0	0.0	0.0	0.0	0.0	0.0
0.0	0.0	0.0	0.0	74.3	34.4	72.8	28.5
0.0	0.0	0.0	0.0	57.1	25.7	71.4	33.3
0.0	0.0	0.0	0.0	76.1	40.1	81.9	37.0
0.0	0.0	0.0	0.0	0.0	0.0	0.0	0.0
0.0	0.0	0.0	0.0	0.0	0.0	0.0	0.0
0.0	0.0	0.0	0.0	68.1	37.9	69.4	31.8
0.0	0.0	0.0	0.0	82.3	70.6	0.0	0.0
0.0	0.0	0.0	0.0	0.0	0.0	0.0	0.0
0.0	0.0	0.0	0.0	0.0	0.0	0.0	0.0
0.0	0.0	0.0	0.0	0.0	0.0	0.0	0.0
77.9	69.7	81.0	68.0	0.0	0.0	0.0	0.0
0.0	0.0	0.0	0.0	0.0	0.0	0.0	0.0
0.0	0.0	0.0	0.0	80.6	48.7	81.3	31.6
77.1	64.1	77.9	70.5	0.0	0.0	0.0	0.0

ABOUT THE AUTHORS

LANCE T. IZUMI, J.D.

Lance Izumi is Koret Senior Fellow and Senior Director of Education Studies at the Pacific Research Institute. He is the author of the highly praised 2012 book *Obama's Education Takeover* (Encounter Books), which details the centralization of education policymaking in Washington under President Obama. He also authored the 2013 PRI report, "One World School House vs. Old World Statehouse: The Khan Academy and California Red Tape."

He is the co-author of the PRI book *Short-Circuited: The Challenges Facing the Online Learning Revolution in California* (first and second editions) and is the executive producer and narrator of a *National Review Online*-posted short film based on the book.

Lance is also the co-author of the groundbreaking book *Not as Good as You Think: Why the Middle Class Needs School Choice* and co-executive producer of the award-winning 2009 PBS-broadcast film documentary *Not as Good As You Think: The Myth of the Middle Class School*. He is the principal co-author of the 2014 PRI studies, "Not as Good as You Think: Why Middle-Class Parents in Illinois Should Be Concerned about Their Local Public Schools" and "Not as Good as You Think: Why Middle-Class Parents in Texas Should Be Concerned about Their Local Public Schools." He also appears in Academy Award-winning director Davis Guggenheim's 2010 education film documentary *Waiting for Superman*, which was voted best U.S. documentary at the prestigious Sundance Film Festival.

In 2008, *The New York Times* selected Lance Izumi to be one of its online contributors on the presidential race and education issues. In 2009, *The New York Times* posted *Sweden's Choice*, a short film on Sweden's universal school-choice voucher system, which he wrote and narrated. Mr. Izumi continues to contribute to *The New York Times'* "Room for Debate" opinion series.

He is also the co-author of the 2005 PRI book *Free to Learn: Lessons from Model Charter Schools*, which was used as a guidebook for creating high-performing charter schools in New Orleans after Hurricane Katrina. He has also authored numerous PRI studies and reports, plus innumerable op-ed pieces in top U.S. and international publications.

For 11 years, from April 2004 to March 2015, Mr. Izumi served as a member of the Board of Governors of the California Community Colleges, the largest system of higher education in the nation. He served two terms as president of the Board of Governors from 2008 through 2009.

(Izumi continued)

Mr. Izumi served as chief speechwriter and director of writing and research for California Governor George Deukmejian. He also served in the administration of President Ronald Reagan as speechwriter to United States Attorney General Edwin Meese III.

Mr. Izumi received his juris doctorate from the University of Southern California School of Law. He received his master of arts in political science from the University of California at Davis and his bachelor of arts in economics and history from the University of California at Los Angeles.

ALICIA CHANG, Ph.D.

Alicia Chang is a cognitive and developmental psychologist (Ph.D., UCLA), specializing in cognitive and language development and applications of cognitive science to STEM education. Since completing her doctorate and postdoctoral research fellowships at the University of Pittsburgh and the University of Delaware, Alicia has been working in the field of education technology. She lives and works in the San Francisco Bay Area, and serves as a researcher at the Pacific Research Institute.

ABOUT PRI

The Pacific Research Institute (PRI) champions freedom, opportunity, and personal responsibility by advancing free-market policy solutions. It provides practical solutions for the policy issues that impact the daily lives of all Americans, and demonstrates why the free market is more effective than the government at providing the important results we all seek: good schools, quality health care, a clean environment, and a robust economy.

Founded in 1979 and based in San Francisco, PRI is a non-profit, non-partisan organization supported by private contributions. Its activities include publications, public events, media commentary, community leadership, legislative testimony, and academic outreach.

Education Studies

PRI works to restore to all parents the basic right to choose the best educational opportunities for their children. Through research and grassroots outreach, PRI promotes parental choice in education, high academic standards, teacher quality, charter schools, and school-finance reform.

Business and Economic Studies

PRI shows how the entrepreneurial spirit—the engine of economic growth and opportunity—is stifled by onerous taxes, regulations, and lawsuits. It advances policy reforms that promote a robust economy, consumer choice, and innovation.

Health Care Studies

PRI demonstrates why a single-payer Canadian model would be detrimental to the health care of all Americans. It proposes market-based reforms that would improve affordability, access, quality, and consumer choice.

Environmental Studies

PRI reveals the dramatic and long-term trend toward a cleaner, healthier environment. It also examines and promotes the essential ingredients for abundant resources and environmental quality: property rights, markets, local action, and private initiative.

The Laffer Center at Pacific Research Institute

Founded in 2012, The Laffer Center at the Pacific Research Institute is dedicated to preserving and promoting the core tenets of supply-side economics. The Laffer Center is named after Arthur B. Laffer, one of the nation's leading economic minds and considered by many to be the "Father of Supply-Side Economics." The Laffer Center houses Dr. Laffer's life's work and seeks-to be the leading source for supply-side research and thought.